The Truth About the Man
Behind the Book
That Sparked the War
Between the States

The Truth About the Man Behind the Book That Sparked the War Between the States

FRANCES CAVANAH

THE WESTMINSTER PRESS · PHILADELPHIA

BOOK DESIGN BY DOROTHY E. JONES

PUBLISHED BY THE WESTMINSTER PRESS®
PHILADELPHIA, PENNSYLVANIA

PRINTED IN THE UNITED STATES OF AMERICA

Second printing, 1976

Library of Congress Cataloging in Publication Data

Cavanah, Frances.
  The truth about the man behind the book that sparked the War Between the States.

  SUMMARY: A biography of the former slave who after escaping to Canada with his family became a well-known minister and active power in the Underground Railroad and served as model for Harriet Beecher Stowe's famous book.
  1. Henson, Josiah, 1789–1883—Juvenile literature.
[1. Henson, Josiah, 1789–1883. 2. Slavery in the United States. 3. Negroes—Biography] I. Title.
E444.H526C38   301.44′93′0924 [B] [92]   75–11566
ISBN 0–664–32572–6

To
My Friends and Fellow Writers
Lois Johnson Becker and Esther M. Douty

Contents

Author's Preface

⌒⌒⌒

"So this is the little lady who wrote the book that made this big war."

The tall President looked down into the dark eyes of Harriet Beecher Stowe, his caller at the White House one day while the War Between the States was raging. She wondered if he spoke in jest, but there was a note of deep respect in his voice as he grasped her small hand in his big one.

The President was referring to Mrs. Stowe's controversial, best-selling novel, *Uncle Tom's Cabin*. It had helped arouse public opinion to such a pitch that the tragic war had become inevitable—the war that would end the slavery she had pictured so vividly.

What Abraham Lincoln probably did not know was that, though the character of Uncle Tom was a composite, Mrs. Stowe gave chief credit to an escaped slave named Josiah. In his new home in Canada, he was better known as the Reverend Mr. Henson, an eloquent preacher who had helped to found a settlement for other fugitives, started a lumber business to aid the settlers, and frequently spoke at antislavery meetings in New England.

Josiah Henson could not have been more different from the stereotype "Uncle Tom," as the term is used today. This negative image came not so much from Mrs. Stowe's novel as from the playwrights and actors who helped themselves to her material in a day when dramatic rights were not protected by copyright. The popular "Tom shows" doubtless helped the antislavery cause but distorted the book. Actors frequently played the chief character for laughs, changing him into a servile flunky. Mrs. Stowe would have been appalled to find that "Uncle Tom" has become a term of reproach.

The true story of the remarkable man who was the chief prototype for her hero might have served as a model for a tale by Horatio Alger. Unlike Mrs. Stowe's hero, who died a martyr's death, Henson lived to be ninety-three, maintaining his zest for living to the end. The modest two-story frame cottage where he spent his last forty years is preserved as the Uncle Tom's Cabin Museum in Dresden, Ontario.

Several versions of the Henson autobiography were published at intervals between 1849 and 1881.

Since the former slave had not learned to read or write until he was in his forties, his books had to be dictated. Descriptions of events sometimes varied, depending on Henson's interviewer. Numerous other sources were consulted. Out of a mass of reading, there emerged for this writer the portrait of a man of great charisma who proved that only in freedom can a gifted person realize his true potential.

"The real history of Josiah Henson," said Mrs. Stowe, "in some points goes beyond that of Uncle Tom in his heroic manhood."

This life story of Josiah Henson grew out of my article, "Meet the Real Uncle Tom," published in 1972 in the *Christian Herald,* portions of which I have reused with permission. Because of reader interest, I continued my research at leading libraries in the United States and Canada and at the Uncle Tom's Cabin Museum in Dresden, Ontario. There was much, much more to be told than was possible in an article about a man, sometimes forgotten and often misunderstood, who deserves a niche in history.

F.C.

1

A Small Boy Named Si

He was an appealing little fellow, even as an infant. Dr. Josiah McPherson, owner of the child's mother, gave the baby his own first name. For a last name the doctor chose Henson, after an uncle who had served as an officer during the American Revolution. The war was long over when little black Josiah, soon to be nicknamed Si, was born in Maryland in 1789.

He was born not on the McPherson farm but on the farm of a neighbor, near Port Tobacco in Charles County. The jovial doctor was too fond of the bottle, and it was doubtless because he needed money that he had hired out the slave mother to Francis Newman. Mr. Newman owned Si's father, a lighthearted man who played the banjo at merrymakings while the other Negroes danced.

Si's only memory of his father, though, was different. A marriage between slaves was not recognized by law, but Si's father considered Si's mother his wife and the couple loved each other. When a white overseer tried to rape her, her "husband" suddenly became a raging black fury.

13

"My father would have killed him," Josiah Henson said later, when he wrote the story of his life, "but for the entreaties of my mother and the overseer's promise that nothing would ever be said of the matter."

This promise was kept only so long as the danger lasted. For a black man to strike a white man was considered the worst crime that a slave could commit. Si's father was sentenced by Francis Newman to receive a hundred lashes on his bare back. His children could hear his screams in the distance as they clung fearfully to their mother. Her eyes were closed, but the tears squeezed through. She made no outcry, not even when her husband reappeared, his back torn and bleeding. His ear, which had been nailed to the whipping post, was severed from his head. From then on he was sullen and morose. His heart filled with hate, he seldom spoke as the days passed, and he brooded over his wrongs. The owner, Francis Newman, and the overseer feared for their lives, but their problem was solved easily. The slave who had been punished so brutally was sold to a slave dealer from Alabama, and his family never heard of him again.

Kindly Dr. McPherson was furious when he learned what had happened. He demanded that Si's mother be returned to his own plantation. Since slave children were assumed to belong to the mother —or rather to the mother's master—Si and his brothers and sisters went with her. In spite of their terrible memories, they were happy to be together as a family. Josiah always remembered his mother as deeply religious. Somehow she had learned the Lord's Prayer and taught it to her children. The youngest did not understand all the words, but the phrase "Our Father which art in heaven" brought comfort to a small boy whose earthly father had been cruelly used.

Sometimes Dr. McPherson almost seemed like a father or a good-natured big brother. He never allowed his slaves to be struck. Si, who was his special pet, always remembered the months on the McPherson farm as a bright spot in his childhood. The jovial doctor, however, took less care for himself than he did for others. Riding home from a party one dark night, he fell from his horse. He tried to walk the rest of the way but, in a drunken stupor, fell into a creek. It was not even a foot deep, but there he was found the next morning, lying face down in the water. Later, the Negroes who had discovered the body pointed the place out to Si.

"There's where Massa got drowned at," they told him.

Si was saddened by the loss of his master and terrified by the look in his mother's eyes. Now the plantation and the slaves would be sold at auction to settle Dr. McPherson's estate, and the proceeds would be divided among his heirs.

On auction day Negroes and potential buyers gathered around the auction block. One by one the slaves climbed the steps to this small platform to stand beside the auctioneer.

"What am I offered?" the auctioneer called out in a singsong voice.

"One hundred."

"Two hundred."

"Five hundred."

The bids mounted higher, and each slave in turn

15

was sold to the highest bidder. A trader from Georgia purchased Jacob, one of Si's older brothers, but what happened to the others Si would never know. He held tight to his mother's hand, a small boy not yet five, and watched when the older children were led away. Then Si was left standing alone when his mother mounted the auction block. She was sold to Isaac Riley, a farmer and blacksmith from Montgomery County some forty miles distant.

At last it was Josiah's turn. He stood on the platform, looking down at the crowd out of wide, frightened eyes. Riley, who had just bought his mother, stood close by.

"What am I offered—" the auctioneer began, when he was interrupted by a disturbance among the onlookers.

Si's mother rushed forward and threw herself at Isaac Riley's feet. She asked him to buy little Josiah too. Her other children had been sold; at least, she pleaded, let her keep her youngest. Riley's only response was a kick, and she was forced to crawl away.

Si's purchaser was a tavern keeper named Robb, also from Montgomery County. At the time, the child hardly realized what was happening; he only knew that he must get to his mother. He ran down the steps and, for a brief moment, felt her arms around him before he was torn from her grasp.

"The iron entered into my soul that day," he recalled later. It was this quality of "iron" that sustained him throughout a long, tempestuous life.

On reaching his new home, Josiah was taken to the slave quarters and promptly forgotten. The forty older slaves who shared the building left for their work in the fields at daybreak. When he cried for his mother, there was no one to hear. When he was thirsty, there was no one to bring him a cup of water. Sometimes at night one of the men, returning exhausted from his day's work, tossed the little boy a piece of corn bread or some herring. Other than that, no one paid any attention to him, even when he was taken ill. Day after day he huddled on a pile of rags in one corner.

As it turned out, Si's illness was fortunate. When Robb came into the building one morning and saw him, he made a quick decision. If he did not want to lose his entire investment, perhaps he had better sell the child while there was still some life left in him. Besides keeping a tavern, Robb owned a line of stagecoaches and a number of horses. Isaac Riley was a blacksmith as well as a farmer, and a few days later the two men met and struck a bargain. Isaac agreed to buy the child and pay for him in horseshoeing— that is, if he lived. If he died, as seemed likely at the time, Isaac would pay nothing at all.

But Josiah did not die. He was returned to his mother, who shared a crowded cabin with other slaves on the Riley farm. He would always remember "what a blessed change" it was. She had no comforts to offer him, but she gave him love, and he began to feel better.

Within a few months he was strong enough and old enough—so his new master thought—to be assigned his own special chores on the plantation.

2

⚜

"A Wonderful Smart Fellow"

Si's first job in his new home was to carry buckets of water to the laborers in the fields, but within a few years he was doing a man's work. A horn sounded at daybreak to call men, women, and older children to their allotted tasks. Breakfast, which they did not eat until noon, usually consisted of corn bread and a small portion of salt herring. At night another scanty meal was served. Then the slaves, crowded together in their cabins, went to sleep on straw spread on hard dirt floors.

Even "the big house," as the master's home was called, was shabby. The new master, Isaac Riley, was a coarse and brutal man. He was not at all like the kindly Dr. McPherson, and Si had to learn what to do and what not to do to avoid a beating.

One day, though, when he was about thirteen, his curiosity got the better of his discretion. The pats of butter churned in the Riley dairy were stamped with two marks, *I.R.*, and he wondered what they were. A slave boy from a neighboring plantation told him that the marks were the first letters in Isaac Riley's first and last names. Si made some ink out of charcoal and cut a quill pen like the one he had seen his master use. He found a scrap of paper and, gripping the pen between his fingers, he tried to copy the marks he had seen on the pats of butter. Those were the first letters that he ever made, and he felt quite proud.

The practice of teaching slaves to read was frowned on, even in states where it was not actually against the law. But Si's friend was lucky. He drove his master's children to and from school and listened carefully when they talked about their lessons. Little by little he learned to read and spell. He agreed to teach Si, but Si would need to buy a spelling book. To get the money, Si sold some apples that had fallen to the ground in the orchard. The next morning when he was sent to the stable to harness his master's horse, he hid the book in his cap, but the horse was frisky and chose that moment to run away. When Si gave chase across the fields, his cap with the book inside it fell to the ground. By the time he returned with the runaway animal, Isaac Riley had spotted the book.

"What's that?" he demanded.

From the tone of his master's voice, Si sensed trouble ahead. "A spelling book," he said.

"Whose is it?"

"Mine."

"How much was it?"

"Eleven cents."

"Where would *you* get the money to buy a spelling book?"

"I sold some apples out of our orchard."

Riley glared. "So you want to be a fine gentleman,

19

do you? I'll teach you to take apples from my orchard. Pick up that book."

Si saw his master's big cane poised in the air. He tried to dodge, but too late. The cane came down on his head and on his back, then again and again, and by the time his mother found him he had been beaten unconscious. His eyes were swollen shut. When finally he recovered enough to resume his work in the fields, Riley greeted him with a sneer.

"So you want to be a fine gentleman?" he repeated. "Remember, if you meddle with a book again, I'll knock your brains out."

Si did not need another warning. It was not always smart to tell the truth, he decided. Like many others in bondage who had no laws to protect them, he had learned a bitter lesson: Deception was often a slave's only weapon of self-defense.

If Josiah deceived his master, as frequently happened from then on, he did it in what he considered a good cause. Isaac Riley was stingy and certainly shortsighted in allowing his slaves to go hungry much of the time. Many days they lacked the strength needed for the hard work expected of them. Josiah was of a sympathetic nature, and he felt especially sorry for the women. Even when ill, they had to spend long hours in the fields.

To take food from another plantation was considered wrong. There was no excuse for a culprit who was caught and he could count on a beating. Si, however, did not think of it as stealing if he took a pig or a chicken from the Riley farm. This was the usual reasoning, for, as one slave expressed it, "What we take belongs to Massa and so do we."

Josiah also felt justified because those he helped

were in great need. His conscience did not trouble him even years later after he had freed himself from the slave psychology. "I esteemed it the best of my deeds," he said. "It was my training in the luxury of doing good."

Whatever hardships Si had to endure, they never dampened his high spirits. By the time he was fifteen he could run faster, jump higher, and wrestle and dance better than any man on the plantation. He was not tall, but he was husky. He smiled often and could see the funny side of almost any situation. When the other slaves were downhearted, they could count on Josiah Henson to cheer them up.

"In those days I had a merry time," he remembered. "Slavery did its best to make me wretched, but, along with memories of miry cabins, weary toil under the blazing sun, curses and blows, there flock in others, of jolly Christmas times, dances before old massa's door for the first drink of eggnog, extra meat at holiday times. The God who makes the lambs gambol, the kittens play, the birds sing, and the fish leap gave me a light and joyous heart."

Si did not mind at all when he was called "a wonderful smart fellow." He had a hard inner core of pride that made him want to excel not only in sports but in work. When Si was eighteen, Riley decided to save the salary of a white overseer and let Si supervise the field hands. This proved to be a wise move. Josiah was both popular and efficient. Under his leadership his fellow slaves worked harder than they had ever worked under threats and frequent application of the lash. And they produced more abundant crops.

Fortunately for Josiah Henson, he did not have to form his opinions of white people entirely from Isaac

21

Riley. He would always have tender memories of Dr. McPherson. Another man who was to have an even greater influence in his life was John McKenny, a baker who lived in Georgetown a few miles away. McKenny owned no slaves. When he could not find free laborers to help in his bakery, he did all the work himself. He also was a preacher. One Sunday morning Si's mother learned that the baker was to hold a meeting at Newport Mill four miles away.

"Son," she told Josiah, "I want you to ask master to let you go down and hear the preaching."

Si hesitated. Once before he had been beaten for making such a request. Then he glanced at his mother, a thin woman, her shoulders stooped and looking old before her time. After working six days in the fields she was too tired to walk four miles, but if Si would go he could tell her what the preacher said. He knew how much religion meant to her, and he could not resist the look of longing in her eyes. He agreed, but he approached the big house with slow, reluctant steps.

"What do you want?" Isaac Riley asked curtly.

"I want to go to the meeting down at Newport Mill, sir."

"Who is going to preach?"

"Mr. McKenny."

"McKenny! What do you want to hear him preach for? Who put that into your head?"

"My mother."

"Ah, I thought it was your mother. I suppose she wants to have you spoilt."

After some more grumbling, Riley gave his consent, and Si started for the house in Newport Mill where Mr. McKenny was preaching. There were so

22

many places Negroes were not allowed that he did not dare to go in but listened outside the open door.

"For every man . . ." he heard Mr. McKenny say.

The words, repeated again and again, sounded like a refrain: *For every man; for every man; for every man.* The sermon was about Jesus, whom the preacher called "the compassionate Saviour." Jesus loved not only the master but the slave, not only the rich but the poor. He loved all who were persecuted or in distress. As Josiah listened, a sense of relief, then of almost unbearable joy, swept over him, as though he had awakened to a new life.

"The compassionate Saviour loves me," he whispered over and over to himself. "He'll be my dear refuge. Now I can bear all things. Nothing will seem hard after this."

He had no bitter feelings, not even toward Isaac Riley. Walking home through the woods, he felt transformed into a different person.

3

❦

A Terrible Vengeance

Josiah wanted to share with others "those little glimmerings of light" that had come to him. As time went on, Isaac Riley apparently became more tolerant in his attitude, for in the story of his life Si mentioned attending other religious meetings.

Josiah was eager to learn and, though he could neither read nor write, he had a way with words. When he talked to his fellow slaves they listened with respect, and he began to preach to them on Sundays. Because Josiah's sermons made the other slaves more contented, Isaac Riley did not interfere.

During the week Si supervised the field hands. On Saturday nights he acted as body servant to his master when Riley and some of his cronies gathered at a local tavern to gamble and to watch cockfights. One night Isaac Riley had too much to drink and got into a fight with Bryce Litton, the white overseer on another plantation. The neighbors sided with Litton and backed Riley into a corner. They pounded him with their fists. Crockery flew in every direction. Riley, a stout man, usually could hold his own in a fight,

24

but this time he was getting the worst of it. Si, sitting outside on the tavern steps, heard his master call.

"Si, help me. Help me!"

Josiah rushed in. A Negro did not dare to raise his hand against a white man, but somehow he managed to elbow his way through the crowd to Riley's side. In the midst of the scuffle, Litton had a bad fall. He too was drunk, but he claimed that Si had tripped him. He threatened vengeance, but, at the time, Si paid no attention. He was too busy dragging his enraged master outside and helping him into the Riley wagon. They drove off through the darkness, but no word of thanks came from Riley, who had been saved from a severe beating.

Josiah had forgotten all about Litton and his threats a few days later when he rode his horse past the overseer's farm. The overseer was talking with three Negroes in an adjoining field; still Si thought nothing of it. But on Si's return along the same road, Litton was sitting on the fence waiting. He rushed forward and seized the horse's bridle. Two of the slaves jumped out from behind some bushes where they had been hiding. The third Negro vaulted over the fence just behind Si. He was cornered.

"Get off that horse," Litton snarled.

"Why, sir?" Si wanted to know.

"To take the worst flogging you ever had in your life, you black scoundrel."

Though forced to dismount, Si tried to keep the horse between himself and the men waiting to attack him. Suddenly Litton raised a stick and the frightened animal ran off, preventing any means of escape. Si, seized by the three Litton slaves, was unable to move. The overseer picked up a fence rail and struck

25

him again and again. Josiah could feel the bones crack as both shoulder blades were broken. The blood gushed from his mouth. Litton, his thirst for vengeance finally satisfied, turned to the three slaves.

"Didn't you see the nigger strike me?" he demanded.

The slaves hesitated, but they were too terrified not to agree. "Yes, sir," they said, and Josiah was left lying in a pool of blood.

When the horse returned without a rider to the Riley farm, Riley set out to investigate. He was furious when he learned what had happened and rode over to the Montgomery County courthouse to swear out a warrant against Bryce Litton. When the case came to trial, Litton swore that Si had "sassed" and attacked him. He claimed that without the help of his own Negroes he might have been killed. Since no black man's testimony was admitted in a court of law, Si's version of what had happened never became a part of the record. Litton was acquitted, and Riley was obliged to pay the court costs. His only satisfaction came from calling Bryce Litton a liar and a scoundrel.

Back at the Riley plantation, Miss Patty, the owner's sister, put Si's arm in splints and bound up his back. She did the best she could, which was little enough, but no physician was ever called. His mother's visits were Josiah's only comfort during the next five months. He had not realized that anyone could suffer such pain. He was left so badly crippled that never again would he be able to raise his arms above his head.

"In time I was able to perform many of the farm labors with considerable efficiency," he wrote later,

26

"but the free, vigorous play of the muscles of my arms was gone forever."

When Si finally returned to work, he became overseer again. He was proud and pleased the first day Isaac Riley sent him to market in Washington, the nation's capital, twelve miles away. Though he never had been taught arithmetic, he was able to get good prices for the fruits and vegetables in his wagon, and he made a strict accounting of every dollar he received.

He was less strict in reporting on the food he distributed among the slaves. Doubtless one reason they worked better under his direction was that they had more to eat.

When Josiah was twenty-two he fell in love. Charlotte, "pious and kind," as he described her, belonged to a neighboring family. They met at a religious meeting and wanted to get married.

Even though there were no legal marriages between slaves, a ceremony was usually performed. If a black preacher was not available, the master might read a passage from the Bible, then hold a broomstick across the open cabin door. The couple would jump across, and "jumping the broomstick" became a symbol of their union. If a minister conducted the service, he sometimes substituted other words for "until death do us part." Instead, he might say, "till death or distance do us part," or "as long as circumstances will permit."

A couple usually realized that the time might come when a master would decide to sell one or the other. Even men of goodwill, who sincerely wanted to keep slave families together, might die, as had been the case with Dr. McPherson. Slaves then

27

would be sold to settle an estate, and a new owner might be less compassionate.

Josiah left no record of the ceremony that united him and Charlotte. They considered themselves husband and wife, and to them that was all that mattered.

4

⁓⁓⁓

Josiah Learns More
About the World

Josiah Henson and Charlotte found their happiness
in each other. They were even happier after their
sons, Tom and Isaac, were born, and later two other
boys, little Josiah and Peter, were added to the
family. The Henson children were fortunate in having a father whose natural shrewdness and inquiring
mind helped to make up for a lack of formal education. Mr. Riley depended on him more and more,
until the selling of the farm produce was left entirely
in his hands.

Most slaves, unless they were sold south, seldom
were permitted to travel more than a few miles from
their own neighborhood. Si's outlook was broadened,
as time passed, by his frequent trips to market. On
the road to Washington, he passed houses much
larger and better kept than the Riley home. He could
almost forget the persistent pain in his shoulders as
his wagon rolled down Pennsylvania Avenue. The
broad, tree-shaded street was dusty, but Josiah was
used to dust. He was much more impressed by the
wonders of what seemed to him a big city, with nine

thousand people all living in the same place. Before he started coming to Washington, he had never realized there were that many people in the world.

One morning he brought his wagon to a halt under one of the trees on Pennsylvania Avenue. As he arranged his fruits and vegetables in neat rows ready for sale, he was interrupted by a question.

"How much are those delicious-looking peaches?"

Si turned to see a middle-aged white man in a long-tailed coat, ruffled shirt, and a tall hat examining the fruit.

"I don't believe I've seen your wagon before," the man went on. "Is this your first trip to Washington?"

"No, sir, not the first, but—" Josiah had several questions which he had been afraid to ask before.

The white man noticed his confusion. "Yes?" he said encouragingly.

"Those big buildings, sir, at each end of this street—" Again Josiah hesitated. "What are they for?"

"The large sandstone house toward the west is where the President lives," the man explained kindly. "The building at the other end of Pennsylvania Avenue is the Capitol. It is still not finished, as you can see. On one side is a big room where the House of Representatives meets. That is where I work. I am a Representative from Connecticut. The room on the north side of the Capitol is for the Senate, two Senators from each state. Together the House and the Senate are called the Congress and make the laws."

"For Maryland, sir?"

"No, for the entire nation. Maryland is only one of seventeen states in the Union. Soon we expect there will be more."

30

This was news to Si. He realized that he lived in Maryland. Isaac Riley had a brother named Amos in Kentucky. Slaves frequently were sold "down South." And that was about all that Josiah Henson knew about the world.

From then on, every market day he never lacked for customers. They talked of places he had never heard of—New York and New Jersey, Pennsylvania and Massachusetts, and other states. He also noticed the way some of his customers spoke. Mr. Riley's cronies, like the Negroes on the plantation, slurred their words. The speech of Si's new acquaintances was more precise.

"I came in contact with many of the most intelligent gentlemen in Washington," he wrote in his autobiography. "They manifested a great interest in me. I listened carefully when they talked and remembered their phrases and sentences. In this way I learned to speak more correctly than the majority of the slaves, or even the poor whites of the district. I never said, 'go dar,' or 'gib me,' for I was anxious to imitate those whom I respected as gentlemen."

Not all of Josiah's experiences were pleasant. He was saddened by one sight that soon became familiar. On nearly every trip he encountered coffles of slaves. Sometimes as many as thirty men, walking two by two, were chained to a longer chain extending the length of a long line. They were closely guarded by slave drivers carrying whips. Women and children either rode in wagons or walked. Fear, anger, but most of all despair, were written on their faces as they began their long journey southward. Slave-breeding in Maryland and other border states had

On Washington trips Josiah was saddened
by encounters with slave coffles

become a profitable business in supplying the demand for labor in the cotton fields of the Deep South.

Si remembered his mother's grief when her children had been sold away from her. Yet she, like most of the plantation workers who had been born in bondage, took it for granted that black people should be slaves. In Washington, however, Si met Negroes who were free. They, or their parents before them, had purchased their freedom. Masters frequently permitted their slaves to earn money by letting them "hire out" their spare time. Or they were allowed to use a small plot of land where they could raise vegetables to sell. Isaac Riley was not that generous, but Si was an optimist. He made up his mind that one day, somehow or other, he would find a way to buy liberty for himself and his family. It would not be easy, but being a slave was not easy. Certainly, he thought with a shrug of his shoulders, it was not easy to please Miss Mathilda, his master's new wife.

At forty-eight, Isaac Riley married Mathilda, a young woman of eighteen. She and her younger brother, Francis, brought with them some property, and Isaac was made the boy's guardian. The new Mrs. Riley was even more stingy than her henpecked husband, and Si was frequently the victim of her miserly and querulous disposition.

In order to reach the market by early morning, he loaded his wagon the night before and began his journey shortly after midnight. Late in the afternoon, he returned exhausted, but she only fretted because he had not received higher prices for the farm produce. When he overheard her complain to her husband, he was afraid that her constant whining would make life even more burdensome.

33

Like most ignorant people, Mathilda Riley was superstitious, and Si took advantage of this weakness. He held up a little ball that, he assured her, would answer questions. The ball was suspended from a slender string that he held in his fingers. From the distance of a few feet, the string was hardly visible.

"So Missus Riley thinks I did not get enough for her butter?" Josiah asked.

Up came the ball, apparently without being touched. But if he asked whether he could have obtained a higher price, the ball would plunge downward.

"Why, it knows everything," Mathilda Riley exclaimed.

The trick seemed to work. At least she did not complain quite so much about the money Josiah brought home from market. But she was still a miser to her brother Francis. To make matters worse for the lonely boy, he suspected that his guardian was cheating him. In his distress he turned to Josiah Henson.

"Master Frank would come to me with tears in his eyes," Si recalled later, "to tell me that he could not get enough to eat. I made him my friend for life, by sympathizing with him and sharing with him the food I took care to provide my own family."

It was during this period in Josiah's life that the United States went to war against Great Britain. Early in the War of 1812, United States forces invaded Canada. In August, 1814, a British army marched into Washington and set fire to a number of public buildings. The first time that Josiah went to market after the British had left, a pall of smoke still clouded the sky. The Capitol and the Treasury had been gutted by fire, and of the house where the President had lived, only the cracked and blackened walls remained standing. The following year the war came to an end, without victory for either side, but it had one unforeseen result.

Black soldiers returning to their Southern homes brought news of states farther north that had abolished slavery. Though slaves had tried to escape from time to time, few had succeeded. Often they were followed by hired slave catchers and sent back to their old masters. According to men who had fought in Canada, there was a British colony far to the north that was a safer haven for runaway slaves than any part of the United States. Once an escapee crossed the border, the laws of another country protected him, and neither master nor slave catcher could force him to return.

Some of the Negroes in Maryland and other border states began to talk of "lighting out." Josiah listened to such talk with mixed feelings. Much as he yearned for freedom, he felt that it would not be honorable to run away. Old habits are hard to overcome, and, from the time he could remember, he had been taught that he belonged to his owner. To take a chicken from the man who owned him was one thing. But a slave was worth a considerable sum of money and must be purchased like any other piece of property. Even some men of religion preached that it was a slave's duty to obey and respect his master.

It was hard to respect Isaac Riley, yet Si felt sorry for him. A relative who also lived in Montgomery County charged him with dishonesty in the management of some property of which Riley was a trustee.

35

Early in 1825 he had to appear in court to defend himself. One night after the final day of the trial, he came to see Si in his cabin. As he sank into a chair beside the fire, he looked so wretched that Si was startled.

"Sick, Massa?" he asked.

The only answer was a moan.

"Anything I can do, Massa?"

"Oh, Si, I'm ruined, ruined, ruined."

"But how, Massa? Why?"

Isaac Riley let out an oath. "I lost my case in court, that's why. In two weeks most of my property will be put up for sale to satisfy my creditor. You know what that means. My Negroes will have to go too. There will be an auction—"

He paused. Josiah realized that if his family was put on the auction block, it was unlikely that all of them would be sold to the same master. A tearful Isaac Riley now made his next move. He rose and threw his arms around the man who had served him faithfully for thirty years.

"I raised you, Si," he said. "I made you overseer. I know I abused you, but I didn't mean it. Promise me you'll do it."

"Do what, sir?"

"I want you to run away to my brother Amos in Davies County, Kentucky, and take all my Negroes with you."

Josiah was appalled. "Kentucky, Massa? Kentucky? I don't even know the way."

"Oh, for a smart fellow like you, it will be easy. I'll give you a pass and tell you what to do."

Riley's plan, as soon as he could settle matters in Maryland, was to follow his slaves to Kentucky. But the Negroes must leave at once! Though it was mid-winter, Josiah was expected to convoy eighteen slaves, besides his own family, through unfamiliar territory to a destination nearly a thousand miles away. Josiah was flattered to be trusted with such an undertaking, yet he hesitated. Riley talked for several hours, appealing to Josiah's sympathy, his pride, and his fears. Soon the county sheriff would seize all the slaves on the plantation, he pointed out. Families would be separated when they were offered for sale. Terror now gripped Josiah Henson. Whatever difficulties lay ahead, he and Charlotte and the boys must stay together.

"All right, Massa," he promised. "I will do my best."

Isaac Riley was no longer tearful. He smiled slyly. As a henpecked husband he had been amused by the clever way Si had manipulated ball and string to play a joke on Mrs. Riley. As Si's master for thirty years, he was convinced that his most efficient slave could be counted on to keep his word.

Josiah was anxious, yet stirred by a strange inner excitement. He had no way of knowing what lay ahead. But he was to learn more, much, much more, about the world—a world which, on that cold winter night in 1825, he did not even know existed.

5

⚜

Decision and Regret

Preparations had to be made quickly. Probably Josiah's hardest task was to tell his mother good-by. Not that he was concerned about leaving her on the plantation. She was too feeble for anyone to want to buy her, so she would be safe. But would he ever see her again, he wondered, as he gave her a final embrace.

Two nights after Isaac Riley made his strange request, Josiah and his slave companions set out on a journey that was to last for about two months. The men went on foot. The children rode in a wagon that held food supplies. Sometimes the mothers rode with the children, sometimes they walked, but no one walked in chains.

Frequently they encountered coffles of slaves. Chained together to prevent escapes, they traveled from dawn until dark, with little chance to rest. Exhausted from their long march, fearful of the future, grieving for loved ones left behind, the Negroes often found comfort in song. Josiah never forgot how they clanked their chains to keep time with their voices as they sang:

When I was down in Egypt's land,
Close by the river,
I heard one tell of the Promised Land,
Down by the riverside.

Cheer up, cheer up, we're gaining ground,
Down by the river,
Old Satan's kingdom we'll pull down,
Down by the riverside.

Shout, dear children, for you are free,
Down by the river,
Christ has brought to you liberty,
Down by the riverside.

Slave drivers realized that singing made their charges easier to handle. But if one of them showed signs of revolt or lagged behind, there was always a whip to make him hurry.

Josiah carried no whip, and he had no fear that any of his friends would try to run away. They trusted him. Moreover, the move to Kentucky seemed to offer a degree of safety. Had they remained in Maryland, their families undoubtedly would have been broken up and sold at public auction to help satisfy their master's creditor.

The procession excited considerable curiosity. Other slaves they met were kept chained, even while they slept. The overseers in charge were amazed to see the Riley Negroes walking about at will. Tavern keepers demanded that Josiah tell them to whom he belonged and where he was going. Any white man had the legal right to challenge any Negro not in the company of another white man. Again and again Josiah had to show his pass, stating that he was authorized to conduct the Riley slaves to Kentucky.

Nearly every night they stopped at one of the inns along the way. It was so unusual for a Negro to convoy other Negroes that the white travelers stared in amazement. Sometimes they invited Josiah to join them in the barroom.

"You must be quite smart," they told him. "Do you think your master would be willing to sell you?"

Though flattered by the unaccustomed praise, Josiah would shake his head. The next morning he and his companions would resume their journey.

He had less difficulty than he had expected finding the way. Innkeepers gave him directions, and when he reached the town of Cumberland in western Maryland, he and his party traveled along the National Pike. This wide highway that led across the mountains had been authorized by Congress only a few years earlier. Already it was crowded with white pioneer families. Some rode in wagons, others trudged along on foot on their way to start new homes in new settlements farther west.

When at last Si and his companions reached the town of Wheeling on the east bank of the Ohio River, he followed Isaac Riley's instructions and sold the horse and wagon. He now had enough money to buy a large boat for the final lap of their journey. The men took turns at the oars, but the Ohio was a smooth, placid river, and no one had to work hard. The wooded shores were lightly touched by spring, and it was April when Josiah and his charges reached Cincinnati. When they stopped to rest, they were soon surrounded by a crowd of Negroes. Ohio was a free state. True, there were "Black Laws" that required every free Negro to carry a pass, and fugitives from slave states were subject to arrest. But in 1825, the Black Laws were not rigidly enforced.

"You will be safe to stay here with us in Cincinnati," one of the free Negroes told the slaves. "Or you can go farther north if that is what you want."

"You'd be fools," a second Negro spoke up, "to go on to Davies County and be slaves to a new master. Don't you want to be free?"

To some of the Riley Negroes, liberty was a new and enticing idea. "Sure, and this is our chance," said one of them. "I'm going to light out for that place called Canada."

"Not me," said another of the slaves. "I'll stay right here and get a job. Then I'll look across the river to that place called Kentucky and laugh my head off every time I think of that Massa Amos. What you aim to do, Si?"

No one in the group yearned for freedom more than Josiah Henson. He wanted to live where his family could have their own house, work on their own land—a place where they could not be abused. Now his fellow slaves were looking at him, waiting for his answer. For a moment he felt his resolution weaken, but not for long. He declared it would not be honest to run away. He had promised Master Isaac to deliver himself and his charges to the brother in Kentucky, and he intended to keep his word.

"We must push on now," he said with a heavy heart. "Everyone back to the boat."

The other slaves looked at one another uneasily. "This is our chance, Si," one man repeated, "and we aim to take it. We ain't going to Kentucky, and you can't make us."

"We ain't going! We ain't going!" The words sounded like an angry chorus as several others took

41

up the cry. Josiah feared he had a rebellion on his hands until one of the women came to his defense.

"Si has always been good to us," she pointed out. "He knows what's best to do. We can trust him."

Some of the other women agreed. "We can trust Si," they said.

The words cut him like a knife but had a calming effect on the men. They continued to grumble, but they liked Si and they were accustomed to obey. Reluctantly they climbed back into the boat. As it pushed off into the stream, they could hear the curses and hoots of disgust from the free Negroes on shore.

Josiah's resolve to keep his word, even though it meant a return to slavery for both himself and others, was almost a religious scruple. It would cause him much anguish in days to come, but the slavery system imposed fetters on the mind as well as on the body. At the time, he thought he had chosen the only honorable course, yet even then he had nagging doubts. Had he also been influenced by his vanity?

"I had undertaken a great thing," he admitted when, years later, he wrote about his decision. "I thought it would be a feather in my cap to carry it through. I had often painted the scene in my imagination of the final surrender of my charges to Master Amos and the immense admiration with which he would regard me."

Amos Riley, of Davies County, Kentucky, was more prosperous than the Maryland brother. He owned several times as many slaves. The "big house" five miles from the Ohio River was more comfortable than the house where Isaac Riley lived, and the Maryland slaves found their situation much improved. Food was plentiful. Josiah and his family had a cabin near the river. From the riverbank they could look across the wide sweeping waters to the free state of Indiana. Like his brother, Master Amos soon recognized Si's efficiency and made him overseer of the five farms that made up the plantation. Si rode from one farm to another and supervised the labor of the slaves belonging to both brothers.

Life in Kentucky brought him new duties and more privileges as well. He now had an opportunity to attend religious camp meetings that were held in the neighborhood from time to time. He heard both black and white ministers preach, and he himself began to preach again, as he had done in Maryland. Though he lacked any knowledge of theology, he spoke with a sincerity that moved his listeners. By observation and practice, he learned how to appeal to a congregation. He listened carefully to experienced preachers. He noticed how they paused to emphasize a point. Sometimes they spoke softly, at other times their voices rose to a high pitch of excitement. He watched their gestures. He took every opportunity that came his way to improve his sermons. In three years he was admitted as a minister in the Quarterly Conference of the Methodist Episcopal Church.

In Maryland, Josiah had come under the influence of John McKenny of Georgetown. In Kentucky, he had a white neighbor, St. Clair Young, who owned slaves but was considerate of their welfare. Eventually, "Mr. St. Clair," as he was affectionately called, freed his Negroes. He had a little daughter, Susan, whom Josiah saved from drowning, and they became good friends. Josiah loved children, even the small imp named Dinah, the quick-witted slave girl of an-

43

other neighbor. When Dinah's mistress would order her to finish a task, she would laugh, kick up her heels, and run away.

"Catch me if you can," she would shout.

Other slaves might be whipped for lesser offenses, but Dinah usually escaped punishment because of her comical ways.

Exasperating though Dinah's capers were to her mistress, they were amusing to other slaves. They laughed uproariously at the little black girl's antics—all except Josiah. He seldom laughed after his arrival in Kentucky. He was not at all his old genial self, yet no one guessed that he was haunted by regret. He kept thinking about the day when he had denied his friends their chance at liberty. For himself he still believed he must obtain freedom by purchase. But had he been fair or just to deny his comrades a chance to seek freedom on their own terms?

"In keeping faith with my master," he told himself bitterly, "I betrayed my friends."

He tried to find consolation in the thought that they were better off in Kentucky than in Maryland. Certainly he and his family were better off, and sometimes he almost forgot that he still belonged to Isaac Riley. Master Isaac had assured Josiah that he would move to Kentucky, but three years went by and Isaac had not come.

Finally, in the spring of 1828, Amos Riley received a letter from his brother. Mathilda Riley refused to leave her old home. Her husband was desperate. After the forced sale of part of his property, he had only a few tracts of land left, which he had to cultivate with hired labor. He wanted Si back, and Amos Riley was to give him a pass for the journey. Except for the Henson family, the letter continued, all of Isaac Riley's slaves were to be sold. An agent was on his way to Davies County to arrange for an auction. The increased demand for labor in the Southern cotton fields made slaves more valuable than ever before, and the Negroes would bring an especially good price. The agent had been instructed to return to Maryland with the proceeds from the sale.

Soon after the agent arrived in Kentucky the auction took place. An auctioneer conducted the sale, and, like most men of his trade, he had a thin veneer of wit. A favorite expression was "putting a slave in one's pocket," which meant "to buy a slave." Auctioneers laughed and joked to persuade prospective buyers to raise their bids. His attempts to be jolly were not amusing, however, to the man or woman standing on the auction block.

To Si the auction at the Amos Riley plantation was a vivid reminder of the scene from his childhood when his brothers and sisters were sold. He remembered his mother's heartbreak, and now again he saw children forcibly torn from their parents. He heard their groans and cries. This time he condemned himself for interfering when Isaac Riley's slaves had wanted to escape.

"What would I not have given," he recalled, "to have had another chance. Because of me, my friends were doomed to wear out life miserably in the hot and pestilential climate of the far South. Death would have been welcome to me in my agony."

On that sad day in the spring of 1828 when Josiah watched his comrades march away in chains, he expected to return to Maryland. Perhaps the two brothers had reached a new agreement concerning him, for Amos Riley was in no hurry to give him a pass. He offered no explanation but told Si to return to his old duties. Spring was a busy time on the plantation, and after the sale the slaves who remained were even busier. Riding from farm to farm, Josiah supervised their work six days a week.

On Sundays he preached. The trauma of the scenes at the auction marked a turning point in his thinking, and remorse added a poignant eloquence to his words.

6

∾

Bargaining for Freedom

One Sunday when Josiah Henson preached, an interested listener was a white Methodist minister, a visitor from Ohio.

"You have too much ability to be a slave," he told Josiah after the meeting. "I believe I know a way to help you buy your freedom. But first you must ask Mr. Amos' consent to let you go see your old master in Maryland."

At first, Josiah doubted that Mr. Amos would consent, but that autumn he saw his opportunity. His sense of timing was as good as that of any actor. In a sense he was an actor, as every black person had to be who resented living in bondage. Slaves laughed when they felt like weeping.

"We did it," said one of them, "to keep down trouble and to keep our hearts from being completely broken."

Josiah had a sense of humor to help him through periods of depression and, for all his new piety, he was a realist. He waited until Sunday morning when he gave Amos Riley his weekly shave to make his request. So much depended on having it granted that he was quaking with fear, but of this he gave no sign as he sharpened his razor. Nor did he mention that he hoped to earn enough money to purchase his freedom.

Instead, he said that he wanted to go to Maryland to see his old master. It was now September and the hard work in the fields was over for a few months. When Amos started to protest, he found the shaving brush perilously close to his mouth. Si, determined to "get a good say" before he was interrupted, promised that he would return to Kentucky in time to supervise the spring planting.

Again Master Amos opened his mouth, only to close it quickly to avoid swallowing a generous portion of soapsuds. By the time it seemed safe to speak, any objections he might have raised had been anticipated. Questions he might have asked had been answered.

"He even told me," said Si, "that I had earned such a privilege. A new era in my life now opened up to me."

Josiah was provided with a pass that would permit him to travel to Maryland and back as "servant of Amos Riley." He also carried a letter about which Master Amos did not know. This was from his Methodist friend to another preacher in Cincinnati. When the boat tied up at the wharf, Si looked up toward the hills on which the town was built. He had left there three years earlier with the curses of free black men ringing in his ears, but his return was in sharp contrast. He was warmly welcomed by the white preacher to whom his letter of introduction was addressed.

This preacher introduced him to other citizens. They procured for him an opportunity to preach in several pulpits in the city, and his simple eloquence touched many hearts. His listeners called him "Reverend," just as they did the white preachers. By the time he left Cincinnati, he had earned $160 toward the purchase of his freedom. In Chillicothe he was equally successful, and he gave full credit to the influence and exertions of the Cincinnati minister who had accompanied him.

"By his advice," Josiah said, "I then purchased a decent suit of clothes and an excellent horse and traveled from town to town, preaching as I went. Everywhere I met with kindness. The contrast between the respect with which I was treated and the ordinary abuse of plantation life gratified me in the extreme. Liberty was a glorious hope in my mind; not as an escape from toil, for I rejoiced in toil when my heart was in it, but as an avenue to a sense of self-respect."

Not everyone in southern Ohio was cordial, since the population was divided between proslavery and antislavery elements. Josiah's pass, however, guaranteed his safety, and his contacts were with people in sympathy with his desire for freedom.

"During the bright and hopeful days I spent in Ohio while away on my preaching tour," he recalled, "I had heard much of the course pursued by fugitives from slavery, and I became acquainted with a number of benevolent men engaged in helping them on their way. Canada was often spoken of as the only sure refuge from pursuit, and that blessed land was now the desire of my longing heart."

Finally he had earned enough to buy his freedom,

or so he thought. Even after his recent purchases, he had $250 left. How proud his mother would be of him! How proud he himself felt when he rode up to the big house on his own horse, wearing a new suit!

When Isaac saw the suit, he seemed both puzzled and irritated. The slave was better dressed than the master.

"What have you been doing, Si?" he asked. "You've turned into a regular black gentleman."

Si explained about his preaching, but a vague feeling of distrust made him wary, and he did not mention the real purpose of his visit. He was anxious to visit his mother, but learned that she had died during his absence. Evidently it had never occurred to Isaac Riley that her son would want to know, and it was a cruel disappointment that he would never see her again. A lesser yet keen regret was not to find Mr. Frank on the plantation. Mathilda Riley's brother, now grown, had gone into business in Washington.

Si was further dismayed when his old master demanded his pass and told his wife, Mathilda, to put it in the desk. That pass entitled him to return to Kentucky. Was it Isaac Riley's intention not to let him leave?

"I seemed to hear the old prison gate clang shut," said Josiah later. "But if Master Isaac meant to outwit me, I must find a way to outwit him instead."

On his way to the stable to put up his horse, Si noticed how run-down the farm had become. Later, in the kitchen, where he spent the night, he was disgusted to find it so filthy. He shared it with the servants Isaac had hired to replace his former slaves, and their snores, added to his own worries, made sleep difficult.

50

"I kept awake," he said, "thinking how I could escape from this accursed spot."

Then he thought of Mr. Frank. Would he remember how he had been befriended as a lonely boy? The next morning, after the master had left for the day, Si saddled his horse and rode up to the house.

"Mistress," he told Mathilda Riley, "I am going to Washington to see Mr. Frank, and I must take my pass with me, if you please."

"Oh, everybody knows you here," she replied. "You won't need your pass."

Fortunately, she did not realize how much he did need it. "I can't go to Washington without it," Si persisted. "I may be met by some surly stranger who will stop and plague me, if he can't do anything worse."

"I'll get it for you," Mrs. Riley agreed reluctantly.

In Washington, Si's welcome was friendly and enthusiastic. Mr. Frank, now a successful businessman, offered to ride out to the Riley farm and try to arrange for the purchase of Josiah's freedom. Frank distrusted his brother-in-law who, as his boyhood guardian, had cheated him out of a large part of his property. His own experience made him cautious and determined that Si should be dealt with honestly. A few days later Frank rode out to the plantation.

He reminded Isaac Riley that Si, during his years of faithful service, had paid for himself several times over. Moreover, Josiah Henson was smart. He had his own horse, and he had his pass. If he should decide to "light out," he might be able to reach a free state before anyone could stop him. Why not take advantage of the fact that he had cash to offer for the purchase of his freedom?

Isaac Riley, in need of money as usual, agreed to a compromise. He would give Si his manumission papers for $450. Si had brought $250 with him, and he raised an additional $100 by selling his horse. That left another $100 still to be paid, and for that sum he gave his note, signing it with a cross.

Riley promised to have the papers drawn up in correct legal form. Frank then returned to Washington, confident that he had struck the best bargain possible under the circumstances. Josiah was overjoyed when the precious document was finally placed in his hands.

Now that he was free, he expected to start out on his own after his return to Kentucky. By hiring out his labor, he felt confident that he could care for his family and soon pay off the note. At the moment, though, he had little cash left. He would be obliged to walk as far as Wheeling—a small price for liberty, he reflected happily.

The next morning, as Si prepared to leave, Isaac Riley offered some friendly advice. If Josiah was stopped and questioned on the road, did he plan to show his certificate of freedom?

Of course, Josiah planned to show the certificate. He was proud of it.

"You'll be a fool if you do," Master Isaac warned. "Some slave trader will get hold of it and tear it up. You'll be thrown into prison and sold for your jail fees before any of your friends can help you."

Si realized this might well happen. Free Negroes often were arrested and sold into slavery if they could not produce proof of their freedom.

"Your pass will be enough," Riley went on. "Let me enclose your papers for you under cover to my brother. Nobody will dare to break the seal, for that is a state prison matter. When you arrive in Kentucky you will have your certificate safe and sound."

Isaac Riley placed the manumission papers in a package, sealed it with three seals, and addressed it to his brother Amos in Kentucky. Si put the package in his carpetbag and gratefully told his former master good-by. The purchase of his freedom marked the culmination of all his hopes, and he was in high spirits as he tramped down the road. He wanted to share with others his faith that miracles could happen, and when he reached Alexandria, Virginia, he asked permission of the mayor to preach. He had not known that it was against the law there to preach to slaves, and for making his request he was arrested. The sentence imposed was a fine of twenty-five dollars or thirty-nine lashes at the public whipping post. Since he did not have twenty-five dollars left, he was kept in jail over the weekend until the sentence could be carried out on Monday. Fortunately, he found someone to send a message to Mr. Frank in Washington, and Frank arrived in a wagon in time to pay the fine.

When Josiah left the jail, a number of Negroes had gathered outside. They begged him to preach to them, and looking into their sad, wistful faces he was determined to run the risk. In his own words, he gave them "such a sermon as they had not heard for a long time." Mr. Frank waited anxiously for him to finish, then hustled him into the wagon, and the two men rode hastily out of town.

Several times before Josiah reached Wheeling, he was arrested. Perhaps Mr. Frank had advised him

53

what to do in such an emergency, for each time he demanded that he be taken before a magistrate. After showing his pass, he would be allowed to proceed. He earned some money preaching along the way, and at Wheeling he boarded a boat for the voyage down the Ohio River. Any unpleasant incidents were almost forgotten by the time he reached Louisville.

In Louisville he had to change boats, and while he waited he could not resist peering into his carpetbag. Yes, there was the package enclosing his manumission papers.

In another few hours, he would be able to tell Charlotte the good news.

7

⌒⌣⌒

A Cruel Disappointment

It was dark when the boat reached the Riley landing on the Ohio River. Si walked to his cabin, where the children gave him a boisterous welcome, but Charlotte seemed worried. A letter to Master Amos from his brother Isaac had told about her husband's travels through southern Ohio. She already knew that he had paid Master Isaac several hundred dollars. To her it was amazing that anyone could earn that much money just by preaching.

"How are you going to raise the rest of the thousand dollars?" she asked.

"What thousand dollars?"

"The thousand dollars that you are to give for your freedom."

Josiah could not believe that he had heard her correctly. In answer to his questions, she repeated what Master Isaac's letter had said. The servants in the big house had heard Master Amos read it to his wife. News traveled fast on the plantation, and everyone, even the field Negroes, knew about that letter. It stated plainly that Si had paid $350 down, but the price agreed on was $1,000. According to the letter, Si must pay an additional $650 before he could be really free.

Only then did he realize that he was the victim of a cruel trick. In sending the manumission documents under cover to his brother, Isaac Riley had wanted to make sure that the real terms of the agreement would be kept secret.

What could Josiah do? It would be both useless and dangerous to appeal to a magistrate. No law court would permit a black man to make accusations against a white man. Josiah would probably be sent to jail, and in order to pay his jail fees he might be sold south. Mr. Frank, the one person who could testify about the terms of the agreement, was nearly a thousand miles away. Si could not even send him a letter. The only persons in the neighborhood who knew how to write were slaveholders, and he dared not appeal to any of them.

Si thought of the package in which his manumission papers were enclosed. Fortunately, he had not yet had a chance to deliver it, and he was determined that Master Amos should not get his hands on that precious certificate of freedom.

"Charlotte," Si told his wife, "I have not seen the package with my manumission papers since I left Louisville. They may still be in my carpetbag, but I do not want to look for them myself. I want you to hide them, but don't tell me where."

The following morning Si was awakened by the horn that called the slaves to work. It almost seemed as if he had never been away as he crossed the fields to find Amos Riley. Master Amos, seated on a stile, greeted him cordially.

56

"Well, boy, how's your master?" he asked. "My brother says you want to be free. Want to be free, eh? I think he drives a hard bargain. Six hundred and fifty dollars don't come so easy in old Kentuck. How does he expect you to raise all that?"

Amos Riley grinned as though enjoying a huge joke. Then in the same jovial tone he asked if Si did not have a paper for him.

"I did have such a paper," Si replied. "The last time I saw the package Master Isaac gave me was when I changed boats in Louisville. But it is not in my carpetbag now."

In fact, he added, he did not know where it was. Amos suggested that he might have dropped the package when he got off the boat, and Si obediently went down to look for it. When he came back with a report that the package was not there, the white man merely shrugged. If the manumission papers were lost, they would not do Josiah any good.

"Well, boy," he said, "bad luck happens to everybody sometimes."

Whatever retort may have crossed Josiah's mind, it was not spoken aloud. Master Amos made it clear that he was to return to his old tasks. He would have no chance to earn the hundred dollars that he had agreed to pay Isaac Riley. Certainly the $650 that Amos Riley claimed was the amount of his debt was an impossible sum for a slave in Josiah's position. But experience had taught him the wisdom of keeping silent.

Even in his despair, however, he did not condone violence. Shortly after his return—two years before the Nat Turner insurrection in Virginia—Si learned of a plot of some Kentucky slaves to rise against their masters. He knew how much many Negroes had suffered. Certainly they had a right to freedom, and the evils of the slave system could not be exaggerated. Yet he was convinced that such an uprising would be both wrong and foolhardy.

"Suppose we should kill one thousand white people," he told the plotters, "many of us would surely lose our lives."

Although Josiah counseled patience, few of his fellow slaves were aware of his inner turmoil. Certainly Amos Riley wasn't, and he continued to joke about the money Si was supposed to owe. Then abruptly the joking ceased. Apparently, the brothers were arguing about Josiah. Each claimed that they owned him. After several letters traveled back and forth, they decided the dispute could be settled in only one way: The slave must be sold, and the money must be divided between the brothers.

One spring day, Amos Riley announced that young Amos, his twenty-one-year-old son, was to take a flatboat filled with farm produce down the Ohio and Mississippi rivers to sell in New Orleans. Si was to go along to help dispose of the cargo. But he guessed the terrible truth. He was to be offered for sale to some plantation owner in the Deep South.

"There is only one thing to do," Josiah told Charlotte. "You hid my manumission papers, didn't you?"

"I did just what you told me," she replied.

"Now you go find them and sew them up tightly in a piece of cloth. Then sew that cloth around my body. Having my freedom papers with me may still save me."

Men much younger than Josiah frequently died of exhaustion in the hot, humid cotton fields. Josiah, because of his great physical strength, might be able to survive. But even if he did, he could not bear the thought of permanent separation from Charlotte and the boys. They were crying, a few days later, when they came down to the Riley landing to tell him good-by. Nor could he keep back his own tears. He knew he might never see them again.

Josiah Henson was the only black man on board. Amos Riley had hired an experienced captain and three white laborers for the trip. At the southern tip of Illinois the placid Ohio emptied into the great Mississippi River. To pilot a boat down this wild and muddy river required skill to avoid hidden sandbars and masses of driftwood just under the surface of the water. The Mississippi was unpredictable. Sometimes it was calm. Sometimes a boat, caught in a sudden eddy, would spin around in a dizzy circle while yellow waves washed over the deck.

The men took turns at the helm, Si more often than any of the others. From frequent association with the captain he became quite skillful in handling the boat, and he seemed to have no fear of storms or shipwreck. His real fear, he said later, had been "the storm of passion" in his own heart. For a gentle, compassionate man, a preacher, the violence of his emotions, which he had to keep hidden, was deeply disturbing.

During the voyage the boat tied up at Vicksburg, Mississippi. A few miles away lived a plantation owner who had purchased some of Isaac Riley's slaves at the sale in Kentucky. Young Amos, more easygoing than his father, gave Si permission to visit old friends, but it was a sad reunion.

"They described their daily life," Josiah recalled,

"which was to toil half-naked in malarious marshes under a burning, maddening sun, exposed to the poison of mosquitoes and black gnats. Their worst fears of being sold down South had been more than realized."

Their master, unlike some plantation owners, felt it cheaper in the end to work his slaves to death and then to buy new ones. Some of Si's old acquaintances had died of malaria, and all that the others could look forward to was the same miserable end. Si left them, feeling sick at heart.

That night, taking his turn at the wheel, he kept seeing his friends, their cheeks caved in from starvation and disease.

If he was to avoid their fate, if he was ever to see Charlotte and the boys again, he must escape. But how? he asked himself. Would he be justified in taking the lives of those who might soon make escape impossible?

"I resolved," he said, "to kill my four companions, take what money there was on the boat, scuttle the craft, and escape to the North. It was a poor plan, maybe, as the plans of murderers usually are. Blinded by passion and stung to madness as I was, I could not see any difficulty about it. One dark, rainy night my hour seemed to have come."

Armed with an ax, Josiah crept into the cabin where the other men were sleeping. He saw Master Amos first and raised the ax. He held it suspended for a moment, then let it drop to his side. Whatever lay ahead, he could not bring himself to commit murder.

With a feeling of revulsion, of horror, when he realized what he had been about to do, he rushed from the cabin. How could he, a religious man who had counseled against violence, have considered taking the life of another human being? Young Amos and the white laborers were not responsible for what was about to happen to him. All night, pacing the deck, Josiah was filled with shame and remorse.

It took time to regain his serenity. But the next morning when his companions came up on deck, they little suspected that their lives had been in danger. Not until years later, when he himself told the story, did anyone ever know how sorely the Reverend Josiah Henson had been tempted.

"I thanked God," he said, "as I have done every day since then, that I did not commit that murder."

New Orleans was a picturesque city of narrow streets bordered by tall plaster houses, faded by time and weather into warm tones of yellow, pink, and lavender. In the public square facing the Cathedral, descendants of early French and Spanish settlers mingled with recent arrivals from the North. Negroes "toting" large baskets on their heads passed by, but Si was more interested in the Negroes in the slave market. This was a handsome building where furniture and other kinds of fine merchandise were displayed. The "merchandise" that most of the prospective buyers wanted to inspect, however, were the slaves exhibited for sale. Si turned away with a shudder and hurried back to the flatboat.

There he found several plantation owners waiting to inspect him. "My points were canvassed as those of a horse would have been," he said. But Si was forty years old, and the prospective buyers wanted a younger man.

By now time was getting short. The last of the cargo had been disposed of. The white employees

61

were ordered to break up the flatboat the next day and sell it for lumber. Young Amos booked passage for himself on a steamboat for the return voyage to Kentucky. Before the steamboat left, the white men would be discharged, and Si must be sold for whatever price he would bring.

Meanwhile, Si had been pleading with the young master to reconsider. Amos obviously was having trouble with his conscience. Unable to look Josiah in the face, all he could say was that he must carry out the senior Riley's instructions.

The last night on the flatboat seemed interminable, but it was not only the June heat that kept Si tossing and turning. His thoughts went back, as they often did, to the time in Cincinnati when he had denied his fellow slaves a chance to escape. Now that it was too late, he wondered, as he had many times before, if he had been influenced by a false sense of loyalty. Or was it false pride? It was nearly dawn when he finally fell asleep.

It seemed only a few minutes before Master Amos called him. He was very ill, and it soon became apparent that he had no ordinary case of indigestion. Writhing in pain, he thought he was going to die.

"Stick to me, Si," he begged. "I'm sorry I was going to sell you. Don't leave me! Don't leave me!"

Those three words were to mean deliverance for Josiah Henson, though he did not yet realize it. He finished packing the trunk in which the money from the sale of the cargo was carefully concealed among the young master's clothes. By noon Master Amos, now barely conscious, had been put to bed in one of the cabins on the steamboat. During the next twelve days, as the boat churned its slow way up the rivers,

62

The New Orleans slave market

Josiah nursed his patient, hardly taking time to sleep. In the long watches of the night, he reflected bitterly about the shabby trick played on him by the Riley brothers. Suddenly he felt relieved of any further obligation to them. Once this decision was made, a weight seemed lifted from his shoulders.

If I do not find my way to freedom now, he thought, may God never give me a chance again.

By the time the boat reached Riley's landing on the Ohio, young Amos was better, but still too ill to walk or speak. Some of the slaves on the plantation made a litter of branches and carried him to the big house. His parents were alarmed to see him looking so thin and pale. When they had recovered from their first shock they thanked Si for bringing the young master safely home. A month went by before he was able to leave his room, and then he too joined in the chorus of praise.

"If I had sold Josiah," he said, "I would have died."

At one time those words would have sounded sweet in the ears of the faithful slave. But by now he was determined to be a slave no longer.

"I felt assured," Josiah Henson recalled, "another attempt would be made to dispose of me. Providence had seemed to interfere, but I could not expect such extraordinary circumstances to be repeated. I was bound to do everything in my power to rescue myself and my family from the wicked conspiracy of Isaac and Amos Riley."

8

✤

The North Star Shining

After his return to Kentucky, Josiah Henson thought of little else except freedom. His family's cabin was near the boat landing, and sometimes in the evening he would walk down to the riverbank. In the gathering shadows he could make out the dim lines of the Indiana shore, and as the darkness deepened, he looked up at the North Star shining in the heavens. By following that star, he had been told, eventually he would reach Canada. If he hoped to escape, he knew it must be soon.

The Riley family's gratitude was short-lived. A conversation between father and son, overheard by one of the house servants, had been repeated to Si. He felt certain that he would be offered for sale again at the first opportunity. A journey to Canada meant danger and privation, and it might not succeed. For himself he was willing to run the risk, but he had a wife and children to consider. He could not abandon them.

"They too must go," he resolved. "They too must share with me the life of liberty."

He made his plans carefully before he took Charlotte into his confidence. She was terrified. If they did not die in the wilderness, she felt sure they would be hunted down and brought back.

"We shall be whipped to death," she sobbed.

She begged her husband to remain at home if they were not to be separated forever. He pointed out that their only hope of not being separated lay in flight, but Charlotte was hard to convince. She had never heard of Canada, nor had she seen the fearful conditions that Josiah had witnessed on the Vicksburg plantation. The unknown hazards of flight seemed to her the greater of the two evils.

Nights of argument followed, but Josiah was firm. "Well, if you won't go with me," he told her one Thursday morning, "I am going without you. I'll take the two older boys with me. At least *they* shall have a chance to grow up in freedom."

Exhausted and discouraged, he left to begin his day's work. He had gone only a short distance when he heard Charlotte calling his name. He waited for her to catch up with him.

"All right, Si," she said tearfully, "I'll do whatever you say."

Now his chief problem was the younger children. Tom and Isaac were stout, healthy youngsters, big enough to walk long distances. Little Josiah was only three years old and Peter a year younger. They would have to be carried. Charlotte was afraid that he would never be able to manage with his lame shoulders, but he insisted that he could with practice. He asked her to make a knapsack of tow cloth, with strong straps to go around his shoulders. That night after work and again on Friday evening he tried car-

66

rying both boys, who thought it great fun. The straps bit into his flesh, but he knew that he could manage. He had to.

Si chose Saturday night as the best time to slip away. The next day was Sunday, and Mondays and Tuesdays usually were spent inspecting two farms distant from the big house. He would not be missed until Wednesday. By then he and his family would have a head start before an attempt would be made to pursue them. One other problem remained. Tom, the eldest boy, was a servant in the big house and stayed there at night. Late Saturday afternoon, when Si went to report on his work for the past week, he asked if the boy could visit his mother for a few days.

"She wants to mend his clothes and fix him up a little," was the excuse.

"Yes, he can go," Amos Riley agreed.

"Thanks, Massa. Good night."

Little did the master suspect what a final good-night it was going to be.

"The coast was all clear now," Josiah said later, "and as I trudged along home I took an affectionate look at the well-known objects on my way. Strange to say, sorrow mingled with my joy; but no man can live long anywhere without feeling some attachment to the soil on which he labors."

When Tom arrived at the cabin he was surprised to find his mother packing provisions for a journey. Nor did the other children know until almost the last minute that they were about to leave. Their eyes sparkled with excitement, but their father warned that they must be very quiet as they stealthily made their way toward the boat landing. There was no moon that night, and when they reached the river, they could scarcely see the man who stepped out of the shadows.

It was another slave whom Si had felt confident he could trust. This friend had a skiff ready, and the family climbed in. The stillness was broken only by the soft splash of the oars as the boat was propelled across the water.

The friend spoke in a whisper. "It will be the end of me if this is ever found out. You won't be brought back alive, will you, Si?"

"Not if I can help it."

"If you get caught," the friend persisted, "you'll never tell my part in this business?"

"Not if I'm shot through like a sieve," Josiah assured him.

When they reached the Indiana shore, there was time for only a hasty farewell.

"God help you," the friend whispered and climbed back into the skiff.

As the Henson family huddled on the shore in the darkness, Charlotte was trembling. She begged Si to call to his friend. "If we go back now," she said, "no one will ever know we have been away."

Josiah shook his head, though he was well aware of their danger. They had landed in a part of Indiana where the people were divided in their opinions about slavery. Josiah had his manumission papers with him. If he was captured by proslavery sympathizers, the papers might be taken from him by force. The entire family would then be lodged in jail until they could be returned to Kentucky.

Josiah refused to dwell on such thoughts. What was important was that they put as many miles behind them as possible. They must be hidden in the woods by daylight.

His goal was Cincinnati, where he had made friends during his preaching tour. It was a two-week journey. During the day the runaways hid in the woods and tried to sleep. At night they took to the road again. Josiah's shoulders ached from carrying the two youngest children, and by morning he would be almost too exhausted to sleep. When he did drop off, he would often wake in a cold sweat. It was hard to rid himself of the fear that slave catchers were closing in.

Two days before they reached Cincinnati, the supply of provisions gave out. The children cried with hunger. Though it was dangerous to expose himself in daytime on a public road, Josiah knew it must be done. Leaving his family in the woods, he set out to find a house where he might be able to buy some food. Instead of traveling north, as a runaway slave would be expected to do, he hoped to avoid suspicion by walking south. At the first house where he stopped, a man curtly informed him that he had "nothing for niggers." The man at a second house was equally rude and insulting. Just then his wife, who had overheard him, appeared in the doorway.

"How can you treat any human being so?" she demanded. "We have children, and who knows but someday they may need the help of a friend."

Ignoring her husband's sarcastic remarks, she invited Si in and gave him a plate filled with venison and bread. He put it in his handkerchief and laid a quarter on the table. She refused to take his money. Instead she gave him an additional supply of venison.

"God bless you," she said, and Si felt hot tears sting his eyes as he hurried back to his family.

They had quite a feast, but the venison was so salty that the children became very thirsty. Their father found a small stream, but when he tried to fill his hat with water, he found that it leaked.

"Finally, I took off both shoes," he wrote years later, "which luckily had no holes in them, rinsed them out, filled them with water, and carried them to my family. They drank it with great delight. I have since then sat at splendidly furnished tables in Canada, the United States, and England; but never did I see any human beings relish anything more than my poor famishing little ones did that refreshing draught out of their father's shoes."

When the family reached Cincinnati, Si's white friends cared for them until they felt strong enough to continue their journey. It was "indescribably sweet," Josiah said, "to enjoy once more the comfort of rest and shelter."

Yet he heard news that made him realize it was important for them to be on their way. New Black Laws had been passed in Ohio and were being strictly enforced. Every black man had to post a five-hundred-dollar bond; otherwise, he was suspected of being a runaway slave. White people were subject to fines if they harbored a fugitive or gave employment to a man or woman who did not carry a certificate of freedom. Riots, usually led by illiterate whites, had spread terror in the Negro section of the city. Many blacks feared for their lives.

Already, Josiah was informed, several hundred sorely beset Negroes from Cincinnati had emigrated to Canada. They had founded a settlement which

70

they named for William Wilberforce, the famous English crusader in the movement to abolish slavery throughout the British Empire. In Canada the Cincinnati Negroes hoped to find the safety and freedom that had been denied them in their native land.

In sheltering the Hensons, their kind hosts risked discovery by unfriendly neighbors, but to them that did not seem to matter. They provided the runaways with transportation in a wagon for the first thirty miles out of Cincinnati. After that the family continued their journey on foot, doing most of their traveling at night as before. Through the trees they could see the North Star shining. Their hope lay in following it across rushing streams and mile after mile through lonely fields and forests.

"Blessed be God for setting it in the heavens!" Josiah said. "Like the star of Bethlehem, it announced where my salvation lay."

9

⚜

"I'll Use My Freedom Well"

Miles of difficult travel lay ahead of the Hensons. They had been directed to take a military road built during the War of 1812, but it had been little used. It led through what was then a wilderness to northeastern Ohio, and it now seemed safe to travel in daylight. Josiah, carrying the two younger boys, struggled through the underbrush ahead of the others, when he heard a frightened cry.

"Mother's dying," Tom said, his voice breaking.

Josiah turned back and found his wife lying on the ground. In her exhaustion she had stumbled and was unconscious. He knelt beside her and tried to revive her, but it was some minutes before she opened her eyes. He gave her a piece of dried beef, the last of the food supply that they had brought with them from Cincinnati. Finally, she revived and was able to continue the journey.

By now everyone was hungry. Josiah had expected to be able to buy food along the way, but they had not passed a single settlement, not even a house. Starvation in the wilderness—was this to be the end of their brave efforts to find freedom? Josiah tried to encourage his family with hopes that he himself was far from feeling. He was close to despair when he lay down beside them on the ground to sleep.

It seemed only a few minutes before they were awakened by a long-drawn-out howl, soon followed by a sharper, louder howl close by. The black curtain of the night was pierced by spots of light—twin bright green spots of light. The eyes of a wolf gleamed in the darkness. Another pair of eyes gleamed beside them. The night seemed filled with cruel green eyes.

"The wolves were too cowardly to approach," Josiah said, "but their noise terrified my poor wife and children."

The next day the family had another alarming experience. They saw several young men approaching in the distance. They were Indians. Almost at the same instant, the Indians saw the fugitives. If the fugitives were frightened, so were the red men. With a blood-curdling screech they rushed off.

Charlotte was convinced that they had gone to find other members of their party and would then return to murder them all. The boys were trembling as they clung to their father. He tried to reassure them, though he too was worried.

Yet he saw the humor of the situation. The Hensons had never seen Indians before. The Indians probably had never seen any black people. How ridiculous it would be for them to run away from one another!

Josiah walked resolutely ahead, with his wife and children trailing behind him. They could see dark eyes peering at them from behind trees. At length

73

they reached a clearing with several wigwams. In front of one wigwam stood a tall, stately-looking man, apparently a chief. He stood with his arms folded as though awaiting their arrival.

The chief greeted the strangers in English. Then in his own Indian tongue he called to his young men to come back. They approached slowly, but curiosity gradually overcame their fear. They wanted to touch the Henson boys. The young Hensons were frightened and shrank away with little cries of alarm. "Then the Indians would jump back too," Josiah recalled, "as if they thought the children would bite."

When each group realized that the others were just human beings after all, they became friendly. The Indians fed the Henson family and offered them a wigwam where they could rest and spend the night.

To Josiah's relief he learned that Lake Erie was only twenty-five miles away, and on the other side of the lake was Canada. The next morning, one of the Indians walked with the family through the forest until they came to the path where they were to turn off. After another night in the woods, the Hensons reached a wide plain. In the distance they could see the village of Sandusky and the blue lake beyond.

Experience had made Josiah cautious. Whatever happened to him, he wanted to make sure that his family was safe. He found a hiding place for them in the bushes before he ventured forth alone to investigate.

Offshore, a small schooner lay at anchor. A dozen or more longshoremen were lined up and carried large bags aboard the vessel. The captain of the schooner called out in a rich Scottish burr when he saw Josiah watching from a distance.

"Hollo there, mon! Want to work?"

"Yes, sir," Josiah called back.

"Come along, then," said the captain. "I'll give you a shilling an hour. Must get off with the wind."

He changed his mind when Si came closer. "Oh, you can't work. You're crippled."

"Can't I?" said Si emphatically, picking up a large bag of corn. He walked swiftly toward the vessel and emptied the corn into the hold. The captain seemed satisfied, and Josiah took his place in the line of long-shoremen. Behind him was another Negro.

"How far is it to Canada?" Si asked nervously.

The black man looked at him suspiciously. "You want to go to Canada?" he asked.

It was obvious that he thought Si was a fugitive, but the next moment Si felt reassured.

"Come along with us then," he was told. "We're going to Buffalo."

"How far is that from Canada?"

"Don't you know, man? Just across the river. I'll speak to the captain. He's a fine fellow."

Si confided to his new friend that he had a wife and four children waiting in the woods. A few minutes later he was telling the jovial Scottish captain the same story.

"You're running away, ain't you?" the captain asked.

"Yes, sir," Si admitted.

The captain looked thoughtful. Slave catchers had been seen in the nearby town, and they might become suspicious if a party of six Negroes suddenly emerged from the bushes in daylight. It would be safer for Si to wait for a while. The captain pointed

75

to an island some distance from the shore.

"I'll lay to opposite that island and send a small boat back," he promised.

After the schooner had been loaded, the sails were hoisted. Si watched anxiously as they billowed in the wind. As he waited, he was tortured by doubts. It was growing dark, and still he waited.

"Suddenly, however, as I gazed with a weary heart," he said, "the vessel swung round in the wind, the sails flapped, and she stood motionless. A boat was lowered from her stern, and made for the point at which I stood. My black friend and two sailors jumped out, and we started off at once to find my wife and children."

They were not in the place where Josiah had left them. When he called, there was no answer. With night coming on, the sailors declared they were sorry but they had to return to their vessel. They could not wait much longer.

Josiah was desperate when he happened to stumble over one of his children. Charlotte had felt sure he had been captured and now was leading his captors back to find his family. She was so agitated that she had tried to hide, and, when he found her, she hardly listened to his explanation. Accustomed to living with fear for so long, she was suspicious of the sailors and even of the black man.

They were patient and kind and finally persuaded her that it would be safe to ride in the small boat beached on the shore. A few minutes later, when the boat reached the schooner, the refugees were greeted with cheers.

The contrast between this welcome and the anxiety of the past weeks left Josiah feeling completely unnerved. A man of forty-one, he wept like a child.

The schooner lay over at Buffalo all night. The next morning, the captain gave a ferryman a dollar to take the Hensons across the Niagara River to Canada. He pointed to some trees on the farther shore.

"You see those trees," he told Josiah. "They grow on free soil. As soon as your feet touch that, you're a *mon.* Be a good fellow, won't you?"

"Yes, sir," Josiah promised. "I'll use my freedom well."

The family disembarked on the Canadian shore at a point near Lake Erie, in that part of Canada now called the Province of Ontario. With a joyful shout Josiah hugged his wife and children. He kissed the ground. He rolled in the sand. A group of curious onlookers had gathered, and one man said he must be crazy. Josiah was too happy to mind.

But he also was practical. A stranger in a strange country, he must find work. On inquiry he learned that a Mr. Hibbard some seven miles away might give him employment. He left his wife and children to rest near the place where they had disembarked. Then he walked to the Hibbard farm. Mr. Hibbard knew a good workman when he saw one. He offered Josiah a job and a two-story house where his family could live.

The house was only a shanty, dirty and run-down. Pigs had taken possession of the lower floor. Josiah drove them out and got busy with a mop and hot water. He scrubbed the floors and the walls. For beds he enclosed four corners of one room with logs. Mattresses three feet deep were made of straw provided by Mr. Hibbard. Mrs. Hibbard gave Charlotte some furniture, and she was delighted with her new home.

She laughed for the first time in weeks.

At first Josiah worked for wages. Later Mr. Hibbard let him farm a plot of land for a portion of the profits. Food and fuel were plentiful. He worked hard and saved his money. Gradually his situation improved. Within three years he owned some pigs, a cow, and a horse. To a former slave it was a great privilege to be able to share in the fruits of his labor.

"I felt that my toils and sacrifices for freedom had not been in vain," he said.

10

⌒∾⌒

A Boy Teaches a Father

After Josiah's flight in 1830, other fugitives began arriving in Canada in increasing numbers. Among them was the fellow slave who had rowed the Henson family across the Ohio in a skiff when they had fled the Amos Riley plantation.

"Many a time in the land of freedom," Josiah said later, "have we talked over that night on the river."

Another escapee was a friend from Maryland. On learning that Josiah lived in the neighborhood, he inquired if he still preached. Josiah's new acquaintances were surprised to learn about his preaching tour in Ohio, where he had been known as "the Reverend Mr. Henson."

The fact that Josiah never mentioned his preaching may have been due to pride. Even as a slave he had felt keenly his lack of education. He could not even read the Bible. The plantation slaves to whom he preached had not minded; they could not read either. The educated clergymen he met in Ohio had helped and encouraged him because they recognized his natural ability. Their knowledge, though, had made him feel more keenly his own lack. Now that he was a free man, he was all the more embarrassed. Did he have any right, he asked himself, to preach to other free men?

But preachers were scarce in the Canadian wilderness. Once it was learned that Josiah had been a preacher, he could not refuse requests that he hold services. His religious meetings were attended by both blacks and whites who were deeply stirred by his eloquence. He found it hard to explain his power over his congregations.

"Religion is not so much knowledge as wisdom," he concluded. It was, he believed, a "reflection upon what passes within a man's heart."

Many of his new listeners now called him "Reverend." He inspired them with such confidence that they did not realize he could not read. He kept his secret hidden even from his twelve-year-old son.

Tom was a bright boy, and Mr. Hibbard paid his tuition for two quarters at a school in the neighborhood. The schoolmaster took an interest in him, and soon he was able to read quite well. Josiah liked to hear him read from the Bible. The father had a retentive memory, and after listening to a passage a few times he could repeat it word for word.

"Where shall I read, Father?" Tom asked one Sunday morning, before Josiah left home to preach a sermon.

"Anywhere, my son."

The boy opened the Bible to Psalm 103, beginning with the words, "Bless the Lord, O my soul." As Josiah listened to King David's outpouring of gratitude, he could not keep back the tears. What a contrast his life was now, he reflected, to what it had been under slavery!

Tom handed the Bible to his father. "It is your turn," he said. "Why don't you read to me for a while?"

Josiah did not reply at once. But the open Bible was on his knees. Tom, who had always thought his father knew everything, was looking at him expectantly.

"I don't know how, Son," said Josiah finally.

"You don't know how to read?" Tom asked in disbelief. "Why not?"

"I never had a chance to learn."

"Well, you can learn now," said Tom decidedly. "I'll teach you."

Josiah was proud and grateful that his son had advantages he had been denied. At the same time, he felt ashamed, but the desire to learn overcame pride. He agreed that Tom should give him lessons.

Every evening after that, father and son studied together by the light of a pine knot. The lessons were not easy for a man in his forties who had been working in the fields since dawn. At first the words on the printed page looked like so many little scratches. But he knew that he must be able to recognize and remember them if he ever hoped to learn to read and write.

Before the winter was over, Josiah was able to sign his name and he could read a little.

"This has always been a great comfort to me," he said later.

His new knowledge also made him realize even more keenly than before how ignorant he had been in his younger years. Most of the former slaves pouring into Canada had grown up under the same shameful conditions. In Canada, in contrast to most of the United States at that time, Negroes received equal protection with white people under law. They could become British citizens and vote. The Reverend Henson, now looked up to as a leader, worried because most of the fugitives were too easily satisfied. They were so thrilled with their new freedom that they were willing to work for whatever wages they were offered, and some white employers took advantage of them. The Reverend Henson's sermons, therefore, did not deal exclusively with religion. They also included practical advice concerning the planting and harvesting of crops.

"We must remember," he reminded his black listeners, "that we are living in a new and undeveloped country. Let us benefit from the example set by white pioneers. Instead of always working for hire, let us save our money and buy land of our own."

After three years of working for Mr. Hibbard, Josiah found employment with Benjamin Riseley, who permitted him to call meetings in the Riseley home. The meetings were attended by some of the more enterprising of his black neighbors, who decided to form an association. In time they hoped to buy or rent land on a cooperative basis, raise their own crops, and thus secure the profits of their own labor. Josiah was asked to find a location for a settlement, and in two successive years he explored, mostly on foot, an extensive, fertile region in what is now western Ontario.

On these trips, he was especially impressed by a tract of beautiful virgin forest on the Sydenham

River. It would be an ideal location for a permanent settlement, but the association did not yet have enough money to buy the property. Then the government offered the fugitives temporary use of a large tract of land near the town of Colchester. The land was already cleared for planting crops. They could live there, rent free, until the tract could be sold to permanent settlers.

"It is a good plan for now," said Josiah Henson. "Still, it is not our own land."

He realized that the fugitives might spend considerable time improving their farms only to have the entire tract sold to other settlers with more money to spend. They must never forget their real goal, he told them—a permanent settlement where they could own their own farms, develop industries, and provide a school for the children.

In Colchester and in other towns close by, Josiah Henson continued to preach. At one meeting in Fort Erie he recognized several former slaves in the congregation. He tried to impress on them that, in gratitude for their own deliverance, they were under an obligation to help bring others out of bondage. After the service one young man, James Lightfoot, who had been much affected by the sermon, asked for an interview. His father and mother, three sisters and four brothers, were still slaves on the Ohio River plantation of Frank Taylor near Maysville, Kentucky.

"I have accumulated some property since coming to Canada," said James. "I would gladly spend everything I have if a way could be found for my family to join me. Would you bring them out of Kentucky, Reverend? You were allowed to travel more than most slaves."

83

"Why don't you go yourself?" asked Josiah bluntly.

"If I did, it would go hard with my family. I never told them I planned to run away. I knew they would be asked questions, and I wanted them to be able to say they did not know what had happened to me. My old master probably thinks I am dead. Now if I should go back—"

"Yes, your family would be blamed. I can understand that," said Josiah gently.

"But you could rescue them, even if I can't," James persisted. "No one knows you in Maysville. Would you try?"

Josiah hesitated. He was a free man now. He enjoyed comforts that at one time would have seemed completely out of reach. To go back to a state where he had lived in slavery might mean capture and a return to bondage. Was it wise to jeopardize his own freedom for the sake of people he did not even know? But the Reverend Mr. Henson believed in practicing what he preached. He agreed to visit the Frank Taylor plantation and guide the Lightfoots to Canada.

Before leaving for Kentucky, he asked James Lightfoot to give him some token that his family would recognize as coming from him. James found one of the stones, now polished and shining, that he had collected as a boy in the creek bed near his old home. "This will let my folks know," he said, "that you have seen me and they can trust you."

"Yes, and that you sent me to help them escape," Josiah added. "I'll tell them that I am your friend."

11

⌒⌒⌒

The Mysterious
Underground Railroad

Since Josiah's escape, people had begun to talk in hushed tones about a mysterious Underground Railroad. It had neither rails nor trains and was never an organized movement on a national scale. Instead, it was a secret method of cooperation in several Northern states among dedicated people who aided slaves in their flight to freedom.

The term was first used, it is believed, by a Kentucky plantation owner. In pursuit of some Negroes who had run away, he suddenly lost track of them when he crossed the Ohio River.

"Them fool niggers must have lit out," he exclaimed in disgust, "on an underground railroad."

What doubtless had happened was that some sympathetic family living near the river had hidden the runaways in the attic of their house or perhaps in a barn. This home, among others, was known as a "station." As soon as it was dark, runaways would be taken from one station to another, where kind men and women, including many Quakers, could be counted on to help.

Men who furnished buggies or wagons to drive the fugitives or who guided them along little-known paths were called "conductors." Those who planned escapes were known as "agents." Josiah Henson thought of himself as an agent.

His first journey in behalf of the "Railroad" was long and tiring. Traveling alone and on foot through New York State, Pennsylvania, and Ohio, he finally crossed the Ohio River into Kentucky. When he located the Lightfoot family he learned that they had given James up for dead. Now in their joy and relief, they talked of nothing else. Soon everyone on the plantation knew that James Lightfoot was alive and prospering in Canada.

But when Josiah outlined his plan for the rest of the family to join their relative, they refused to leave. The parents were old and frail. The sisters who had young children did not want to expose them to the dangers of trying to escape.

Josiah could not hide his disappointment. Had his long, hard journey been for nothing? "What about you and your three younger brothers?" he asked Jefferson Lightfoot, the eldest.

"We want very much to go—also my young nephew," said Jefferson earnestly, "but I'm afraid we've talked too much. Now everyone is expecting us to run away, and slave catchers would be after us before we had gone ten miles. As for you—"

Josiah nodded. He realized that if he were caught, he would be sent back to the Amos Riley plantation.

"Later, if you will come for us again," said Lightfoot, "we will be more careful."

Josiah promised, but warned that next time they must take no one into their confidence. Flight was becoming more difficult. Underground Railroad activities made county authorities more cautious, and patrollers kept a closer watch on the roads leading north. Plantation owners hired more slave catchers to pursue escapees even after they crossed the river into so-called "free" states. Rewards offered for information leading to their capture were tempting to poor whites. In the words of one former slave, "They was all kinds of white folks, just like they is now. Devils and good people walking in the road at the same time, and nobody could tell one from t'other."

Even some blacks, for the sake of a few dollars, aided in the return of slaves to their old masters. Fugitives had to be wary about whom they trusted. Yet even the possibility of capture and terrifying stories of punishments meted out to those who were caught could not quench the desire for freedom. Some of the more daring Negroes were willing to risk almost any danger to escape from slavery. Often entire families fled because they were about to be sold and separated from one another. Many fugitive slaves had been harshly treated, but some of those whose masters were kind also felt the urge to get away.

"I've got freedom in my bones," said one.

The difficulty for the majority of slaves was that they did not know where to go. There was hushed talk in the cabins about a mysterious Underground Railroad and a free country "somewhere." But where was it? To men and women kept in ignorance, "the North" was merely a name, and information was even more vague about Canada. The Lightfoot brothers, though they themselves dared not make the attempt at that time, had heard of some other slaves who were anxious to escape, if only they could find a leader to guide them.

Josiah set out at once on a forty-mile hike into the interior of Kentucky. When he located the slaves of whom Jefferson Lightfoot had told him, he warned them to be cautious. They left the following Saturday evening. Walking the roads at night and hiding in the woods during daylight, they reached Cincinnati in safety. Here they were welcomed by kind people who had befriended Josiah before. From Cincinnati their route led northward through Indiana, where there were several Quaker settlements. In Quaker homes the escapees were offered food and a chance to rest. So far, all had gone well on Josiah's first mission for the Underground Railroad.

When he and his companions reached Toledo, Ohio, on the southwest shore of Lake Erie, they took passage for Canada. Some of the fugitives sought out relatives and acquaintances close by. Others went to Colchester, where they were given shelter until they could find work in a new country.

Josiah's fields yielded a good crop that summer, and he was in a position to finance further activities on behalf of the Underground Railroad. His next mission was another attempt to rescue the Lightfoot brothers. The following autumn, after crossing Lake Erie, he walked the entire length of the State of Ohio. He planned to board a steamboat at Portsmouth, and travel up the Ohio River to Maysville.

In Portsmouth, though, he ran into trouble. A group of visiting Kentuckians looked at him suspiciously. They began talking in low tones, and Josiah wondered if they were asking what he, a strange Negro, was doing here. Was he a runaway? Was there, perhaps, a reward for his capture? Before he could be questioned, he hurried off in the direction of some woods, but he could not stay in hiding. He had a steamboat to catch.

"I was obliged to resort to a trick," he said later. "I procured some dried leaves, put them into a cloth, and wound it around my face, reaching nearly to my eyes."

The trick worked. When he reappeared on the street, the Kentuckians surrounded him. Who was he? they asked. What was his name? What was he doing in Portsmouth? Each time Josiah mumbled as though trying to reply and pointed to his face. The assumption was that he had such a bad toothache he could not speak. He spent several anxious hours before the arrival of the steamboat and he could go on board.

It was dark when he reached Maysville. Early the next morning the second person he met on the street was Jefferson Lightfoot. He and his brothers had been waiting for Josiah's return but had said nothing to anyone else, not even to other members of their family. Josiah, on the chance that he might be remembered from his earlier visit, hid in the woods, emerging only after dark to discuss details. The youngest of the four Lightfoots was still only a boy, but he and a nephew were considered old enough to make the trip. By Saturday night they were ready to start.

It was heartbreaking for the brothers to leave without saying good-by to their aged father and mother, whom they might never see again. For the protection of the parents, however, as well as that of the sons, it seemed wise that no one left behind should have any inkling that an escape had been planned. As a further precaution, the Lightfoots had hidden a skiff for the first part of their getaway. Bloodhounds, often used to track down fugitives, would not be able to detect a scent in water. Josiah felt confident that by daylight they would be able to reach Cincinnati, where his friends would give them temporary shelter.

Unfortunately for these plans, the boat sprang a leak. The men waded to shore, shivering in the cold November wind, and continued their journey on foot. At length they reached the Miami River. Not knowing how deep it was, they wandered up and down the bank looking for a safe crossing place. All were in despair except Josiah, who remained cheerful. He pointed to a cow that was approaching the stream as though it intended to drink.

"Boys," he said, "perhaps the Lord sent us that cow to show us where to cross the river. It may be that she can tell us some news."

His companions looked skeptical as the cow waded out into the water. But when it reached the farther shore without swimming, a shout went up from the men. If the stream was shallow enough for the cow, it would be safe for them too. Safe, but very, very cold. Halfway across, the youngest of the Lightfoots was seized with cramps and had to be carried. On shore his brothers rubbed his limbs vigorously before he was able to go on. In Cincinnati they had a chance to rest in the home of Josiah's friends before they set out again.

As before, Josiah chose a route through Indiana, but he knew that he might not be as fortunate as on his first trip. He had been warned about proslavery sympathizers in the state, so he and his companions kept to the woods except at night. The weather was freezing as the little group waded through mud and rain and snow on their long march toward Canada.

They had not gone far when the youngest Lightfoot brother became alarmingly ill. The others made a litter out of branches to carry him, but he realized that their slow progress might endanger the lives of them all. He begged them to go on without him. He appeared to be dying, when Josiah peered through the trees and saw a wagon coming down the road. He chose a bold plan, taking a roundabout course to the road.

"I wanted to make it appear," he said, "that I had been traveling in the opposite direction to that which the wagon was taking. When I came up to the driver, I bade him good day."

The man in the wagon pulled his horses to a halt. "Where is thee going?" he asked kindly.

From the plain cut of his coat and his use of the word "thee," he obviously was a Quaker. Josiah felt a surge of relief and led the way to the hiding place in the woods. The Quaker was moved to tears when he saw the sick boy, and he helped carry him to the wagon. The horses were turned around for the trip back to the Quaker's home, where his wife and daughters put the boy to bed. The others in the party were invited to spend the night. When they left the next morning, the Quaker family assured the Lightfoots that their brother would be cared for until he was well enough to travel.

A few days later a white man whom the fugitives met on the road seemed friendly. Though he was from the South, he said he was opposed to slavery, and he had disturbing news. He had heard rumors about the Lightfoots and slave hunters who were on their trail. By now the fugitives were within a night's walk of Lake Erie, and they arrived just as the first pale streaks of dawn appeared in the sky. Liberty was almost in their grasp when they reached a tavern near the shore. At this distance it seemed safe enough to accept their new white friend's invitation to have breakfast with him.

As the landlord was preparing the meal, Josiah had a premonition of danger. He urged his companions to leave the inn. They were exhausted and hungry, and it was only after his continued insistence that they followed him. No sooner had they stepped outside than they heard the rapid hoofbeats of horses coming closer. They barely had time to hide behind some bushes when several armed horsemen drew rein before the tavern. Their new white friend stood in the doorway, answering questions.

Had he seen any Negroes? the slave catchers asked.

Yes, was the reply.

How many?

About six.

Where had they gone?

The white friend pointed to the road leading toward Detroit, and the horsemen disappeared in a cloud of dust. Not realizing that they were traveling in the wrong direction, they felt confident that the runaways would soon be captured. Josiah and the Lightfoots reentered the inn, where they had a quick breakfast. Then, before the slave catchers had time to realize their mistake, the sympathetic landlord sailed them in his own boat across the lake to Canada.

"Words cannot describe," Josiah said, "the feelings of my companions when they reached the shore. They danced and wept for joy and kissed the earth." Their reactions reminded him of his own happiness when he had first realized that he was free.

James Lightfoot was both grateful and elated to see his brothers. The story was to have an even happier ending than any of them realized at the time. The boy who had been so sick arrived a few months later. He was fully restored to health after being nursed by the Quaker family. Later still, Frank Taylor, the former owner of the Lightfoots, was taken ill. Perhaps because he feared that death was near, he gave the members of the family still in his possession their freedom, and eventually they all were reunited in a new country.

Josiah Henson left a record of two excursions into Kentucky on behalf of the Underground Railroad. There must have been other trips, since it gave him great happiness in later years to recall that he had helped rescue one hundred and eighteen human beings. At the time and for years thereafter, the operations of the so-called Railroad were shrouded in secrecy. This secrecy was a protection both for the runaways and for the people who aided in their escape. Quakers and other conscientious men and women were well aware that they were disobeying an American law. In helping their fellowmen they were convinced that they were obeying a higher law, and they suffered fines and imprisonment when they were caught. "Agents" and "conductors," some of them from the South, ran grave risks, and their activities required courage and dedication.

None were braver and ran graver risks than did those black fugitives who left a safe haven in Canada to go to the aid of others still in bondage. They were the ones who did the most to spread the news that far to the north was a country where Negroes could be free.

A few years after Josiah Henson's escape, a young woman, Victoria, became queen of England. In the 1840's she announced that every escapee who reached her colony west of the Atlantic would be protected by the laws of the British Empire. This announcement gave rise to a popular song, ending with the words:

> Oh, I heard Queen Victoria say
>   That if we would forsake
> Our native land of slavery,
>   And come across the lake;
> That she was standing on the shore,
>   With arms extended wide,
> To give us all a peaceful home
>   Beyond the rolling tide;
> Farewell, ole master, don't think hard of me,
>   I'm traveling on to Canada,
>   where all the slaves are free.

12

⚭

A Town Called Dawn

It was Josiah Henson's good fortune while living at Colchester to meet Hiram Wilson, a young Congregational missionary. Hiram had recently arrived from Oberlin College to work among the fugitives, whose story he found as touching as that of the Children of Israel who had fled slavery in Egypt. He heartily approved when the Reverend Henson talked of starting a permanent settlement for Negroes.

"He took an interest in our people," Josiah said, "and wanted to do what he could to promote the cause of improvement I had so much at heart."

Josiah's idea was still only a dream until a third man entered the picture. The Reverend Wilson wrote to James Canning Fuller, a wealthy Quaker in New York State who was about to leave for England. Fuller knew a number of English members of the Society of Friends, and from them he collected fifteen hundred dollars for the "Canada cause." After his return, Henson and Wilson called a convention in the Canadian town of London, and every Negro set-

95

tlement close by was invited to send delegates. For three days the delegates discussed the wisest way to spend the money contributed by the English Quakers.

"Most important of all," Josiah Henson urged, "is to have a school."

When black fugitives arrived in Canada, most of the natives were sympathetic. Yet here, too, Negroes were sometimes the victims of prejudice. Black children could attend public schools but were often harassed by white schoolmates, and some white teachers objected to teaching them. Henson wanted a school where both whites and any Indians who wished to attend would be welcome, but in which Negroes would be treated as equals. It was to be a manual labor school, one that would provide young people and older ones alike with an elementary education as well as training in the manual skills needed in a pioneer community. A board of trustees, made up of both black and white members, was asked to take charge.

Because of the help received from abroad, this new school in the wilderness was given the somewhat pretentious name of the British American Institute. In time it was expected to form the nucleus of a town. Henson and Wilson were then appointed to a committee to find a site for a permanent settlement.

During the next few months the young man and the older one traveled through the surrounding area. In the end they selected the same beautiful, fertile region on the Sydenham River that Josiah had seen and liked several years earlier. Here on behalf of the Institute's trustees, the committee agreed to purchase two hundred acres of land for four dollars an acre. Josiah, a frugal and by now a successful farmer, had the forethought to buy an additional two hundred acres out of his own savings. Because he paid cash, the original owner of the land offered him a discount. Josiah then sold a hundred of these acres to the Institute at the same low price that he had paid, saving the trustees a considerable sum of money.

"We looked to the school and the ownership of land," he said, "as two ways by which Negroes, once members of an oppressed race, could enjoy and participate in the blessings of civilization."

The new settlement was called Dawn. The name summed up Josiah's hopes and dreams, not only for the new black citizens but for other refugees who were to come.

Money was always a pressing need, and Hiram Wilson and the Quaker James Fuller went to England on a fund-raising tour. They also recommended Josiah Henson as an excellent speaker to antislavery leaders in New England and New York State. For several successive winters, he solicited funds for the new school at meetings usually held in churches. As he stood in the pulpit, the genial smile on his dark face seemed intended for everyone in the congregation. Each of his listeners had the feeling that Josiah was appealing directly to him. The Reverend Henson's eloquence, combined with his simple sincere manner—qualities that today would be called charisma—readily made friends both for himself and for the cause he championed.

In 1842, Josiah and a number of other black settlers moved their families to Dawn. In the shade of tall, majestic walnut trees they built their new town.

The settlers lived in log houses, but their chief pride was the larger log school building for the British American Institute. Though the building was simple enough, the name seemed to give it added dignity. It opened its doors with only twelve pupils, and at first Hiram Wilson was the only teacher.

By the autumn of 1845, several other teachers had arrived, sent to Dawn by churches in Canada and the northern part of the United States. Nearly a hundred students had enrolled.

"We might have three times that number," said the Reverend Wilson, "had we accommodations for them. Our souls are weighed down with sorrow when we have to turn away applicants."

By then, more than sixty acres around the school were cleared and brought under cultivation. Word went out to towns close to the American border that refugees would be cared for at Dawn until they could find work in this strange country. Most of them arrived after a long, hard journey, with no money and with only the clothes they were wearing. Older residents distributed supplies of clothing and provisions furnished by Canadian churches and American sympathizers.

The chief hardship for Negroes, accustomed to a warmer climate, was the freezing Canadian winter. The men kept busy—and tried to keep warm—chopping down trees to clear the land for spring planting. Most of them attended school part of the time along with the children. At night the newcomers huddled around the fireplaces in the long log building where they were housed until they could establish homes of their own. Close by stood the four-room frame cottage where Josiah Henson lived with his family, and nearly every evening the tiny parlor was crowded with visitors.

During the summer months, both Henson and Wilson preached at outdoor camp meetings. The meetings not only furnished spiritual comfort but were one of the few recreations of the time. Stands were erected for the speakers, and booths were set up where refreshments were sold. The Reverend Wilson was an earnest, sincere man, but it was the Reverend Henson, with his wit and sense of drama, who drew the largest crowds. Visitors, both black and white, often came from a great distance to hear him preach.

With the coming of winter again, both men spent much of their time in New England and New York State, pleading for financial aid. And both soon learned how it felt to be mistrusted by people they tried to help. Some of the residents at Dawn blamed them for the settlement's financial difficulties, only to have opposition vanish for lack of evidence.

At one Negro convention in 1847, Josiah was accused of mismanaging the sums he had collected. But he was no longer a slave under the rule of an all-powerful master, and he refused to weaken under pressure. When called to the witness stand, he made a spirited defense and cleared his name. In the years ahead, however, he was to face similar charges by former slaves who had had no experience in handling money. Most of the residents at Dawn loved and respected him, as had the slaves he had once supervised. Others, now freed from the restraints of their former bondage, resented his assumption that he always seemed to know what was best for them. Their antagonism doubtless was tinged with envy of his superior ability, yet some of Josiah's white contemporaries agreed.

"Henson was more than a match for anyone that ever tried to curb his authority," declared William King, a well-known Presbyterian minister and founder of one of several similar communities for Negro fugitives.

Apparently Henson, who had overcome obstacles that once seemed insurmountable, did not realize he might have limitations. If he had, he probably would not have tried to establish a settlement in the wilderness and would not have accomplished what he did. Like Hiram Wilson, he was dedicated to the cause he served, yet, viewed from the distance of more than a hundred years, it would seem that neither was a good businessman.

Of the two, the Reverend Wilson was the more impractical. When he borrowed money, he had faith "in the Lord to find ways of paying." Disappointed and discouraged, he finally moved to the town of St. Catherine's. Here he continued to minister to runaway slaves who crossed the border near Niagara Falls, but he was relieved of the financial responsibility that had troubled him at Dawn.

Henson took a more realistic approach than Wilson. The land purchased was covered by a heavy growth of black walnut and other trees. Some were felled to provide lumber for the schoolhouse and other buildings, but many trees were burned merely to get rid of them so the ground could be cleared for planting.

So much waste shocked Josiah. He made no mention of his plans when he set out on another journey, this time to observe the workings of the lumber busi-

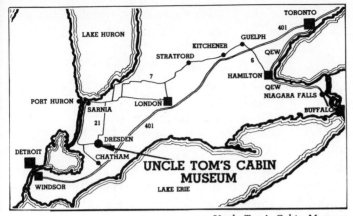

Uncle Tom's Cabin Museum

Henson's cottage survives as a museum
where Dawn once flourished

ness in the northeast part of the United States. In
New York State he visited sawmills where logs were
sawed into planks, instead of ruthlessly destroyed as
they were at Dawn. This lumber, he was told,
brought good prices in New England.

The next step was to raise money to build a sawmill. In Boston he met Samuel A. Eliot, a former
mayor of the city. The sawmill, as Henson outlined
his plan, would not belong to him personally but to
the Institute.

"An excellent idea!" said Eliot. "I have friends who
also may be interested."

Together with Amos Lawrence, a merchant, and
Dr. Henry Ingersoll Bowditch, Eliot contributed
fourteen hundred dollars. Fired with fresh enthusi-
asm, Josiah Henson returned to Dawn. There, with
the help of his sons, now grown into husky young
men, and several others, he began to build a sawmill.

101

By the time the framework was completed and the roof covered, his funds were exhausted and he had no money left to stock the mill with machinery. At this point, the plan seemed doomed to failure, but Josiah seldom gave up. He made another trip to Boston, where his friends—Eliot, Lawrence, and Bowditch—encouraged him to go ahead.

"The approval of such men was like balm to my soul," he said later. "They endorsed a note for me and put it in the bank. I then was able to borrow eighteen hundred dollars more. With this sum, I completed the mill, stocked it with machinery, and had the pleasure of seeing it in successful operation. The mill introduced an entire change in the appearance of that section of the country and in the habits of the people."

The first load of black walnut lumber, sawed in the mill at Dawn, was carried to Boston on a vessel chartered by Josiah Henson. He sold it to Jonas Chickering, a piano manufacturer, and made enough profit to cancel his debt. The three benefactors who had gone on his note refused to take his money.

"You will need it," Eliot suggested, "as working capital."

Josiah was busy, thinking of ways to expand his business and make life better for his people.

Dawn, with its school, a blacksmith shop, a gristmill, and now a sawmill, had grown into a real town. The Henson family also had grown, with the addition of a fifth son and two daughters. What doubtless gave Josiah and Charlotte the most satisfaction was that their children, like other black youngsters in the community, were receiving the education that had been denied the parents under slavery.

In spite of apparent prosperity, however, the Institute was deeply in debt. Problem piled on problem. The different denominations that had helped the school from time to time had also created divisions among the residents at Dawn. This was not too surprising. They lived in an age when different sects often bickered over doctrine, and the fugitives had fled from a country that was wracked by dissension.

Yet the Reverend Henson, more tolerant than many preachers of his time, remained an optimist. Difficulties had been overcome before. To him the future looked bright.

13

⤳✿⤳

Putting Legs on an Idea

Boston, during the 1840's when the Reverend Henson was a frequent visitor, was a city sharply divided between antislavery forces and proslavery sympathizers. In a town where the first voices had been raised against tyranny before the American Revolution, many citizens now condoned the bondage of more than four million black Americans. Though slaveholders represented only a small minority in the South, they were a powerful minority. The invention of the cotton gin had made cotton-growing profitable for both South and North. People who condemned slavery talked about an "unholy alliance between lords of the loom and lords of the lash." The rich planters supplied the New England cotton mills with the raw material grown by slave labor.

Few of the millowners or the mill hands who worked for them, few merchants who sold cotton goods or their customers, had ever seen slavery at firsthand. They knew, of course, that the economy was tied up with cotton, and to oppose the system that produced it in such plentiful supply was a threat to business. Even the "timid good," whose consciences may have troubled them, kept silent rather than defy public opinion.

Then public opinion gradually began to change. More and more people spoke out against slavery, none with greater fervor than a young Boston printer, William Lloyd Garrison. On New Year's Day, 1831, he had begun to publish *The Liberator,* an antislavery newspaper.

"I shall strenuously contend for the immediate enfranchisement of our slave population," he wrote in his first editorial. "I *will be* as harsh as truth and as uncompromising as justice. On this subject I do not wish to think, or speak, or write with moderation. No! No! Tell a man whose house is on fire, to give a moderate alarm . . . ; tell the mother to gradually extricate her babe from the fire into which it has fallen; but urge me not to use moderation in a cause like the present. I am in earnest. . . . I will not excuse—I will not retreat a single inch—and *I will be heard."*

In 1833 Garrison helped to found the American Anti-Slavery Society. The movement spread rapidly through Northern cities, with the organization of local societies. Garrison convinced many Americans who until then had been indifferent that drastic action was needed—and at once. As was to be expected, slave owners detested him. This was true also of many people in the North, although many of them were dedicated to the cause of freedom for the slave. They feared that the radical views of Garrison and his hotheaded followers, called abolitionists, might bring about a civil war.

But there was no stopping William Lloyd Garrison. He condemned the United States Constitution as "a covenant with hell" because at that time it did not forbid slavery. At a Fourth of July celebration in Framingham, Massachusetts, he touched a match to a copy of the Constitution. His eyes gleamed behind his steel-rimmed spectacles as he watched it burn.

"So perish all compromises with slavery," he shouted.

Even some of the people most deeply shocked by Garrison's speeches were aroused to action. Both extremists and moderates were agents and conductors for the Underground Railroad. In Boston and other cities, Vigilante Committees were organized to provide hiding places for runaway slaves or to guide fugitives who wanted to go to Canada. Antislavery leaders were unrelenting in their efforts, and frequent mass meetings won new converts to the cause. It was soon found that the fugitives themselves furnished the best propaganda.

"To make our antislavery idea fully understood," said one white worker, "we must put legs on it."

He realized that an audience bored by an abstract discussion of the evils of slavery sat up and took notice when a black man or woman told of a hairbreadth escape.

One of the most popular orators at these meetings was Frederick Douglass, an ex-slave from Maryland. He was a handsome man whose dignified bearing gave his words all the greater impact when he told an audience: "I stole this head, these limbs, this body, from my master, and ran off with them."

Another escapee, William Wells Brown, who as a free man wrote several excellent books, could hold an audience spellbound. A few speakers, though they might be less brilliant, had their listeners sitting on

106

the edge of their chairs as they told bizarre stories of their escapes. Some of the fugitives had taken flight by clinging to locomotives. Others had ridden logs down swift-flowing rivers, stowed away on ships, or hidden in swamps and haystacks.

"They are among the heroes of our age," said Senator Charles Sumner. "Romance has no stories of more thrilling interest than theirs."

In the need for speakers, Josiah Henson offered his services, and he had a special, personal reason for wanting to help. Not since his brothers and sisters were sold had he known what became of any of them. Then he met an Underground Railroad conductor, William Champlain. On one of his rescue missions down South, Mr. Champlain had met and talked with Josiah's brother Jacob, now a slave on a Georgia plantation. He had offered to help Jacob escape to the North, but unfortunately the Underground worker's activities were discovered. Georgia authorities arrested Champlain and sentenced him to prison until he could pay the excessive bail demanded. Luckily, some Quaker friends in Connecticut learned of his plight. Three of them obtained his release by paying the bail, though one of the three had to sell his farm in order to contribute his share.

Josiah was deeply touched by their generosity. Concern for his brother was mingled with relief that he was alive. A way still might be found to rescue him, just as he himself had rescued other slaves. Whatever Josiah could do to help the antislavery cause must be done, and he accepted many invitations to speak.

Sometimes these mass assemblies turned into rowdy affairs. Visiting slave owners and proslavery sympathizers often attended out of curiosity, hoping for "a good show." When local ruffians tried to break up a meeting, the interruptions only added to the excitement. Abolitionists welcomed hecklers, since they gave a speaker a chance to refute arguments that attempted to justify slavery.

Josiah did not mind hecklers. He was a natural showman, combining the appeal of an old-fashioned preacher with a sense of humor. On one occasion, he was speaking in Tremont Temple, a leading Boston church. Several Southern planters were in the congregation, and he remembered the time he had been refused permission to preach to slaves in Alexandria, Virginia. The memory of his narrow escape from thirty-nine lashes added emphasis to his descriptions of life under slavery. He was wrought up to a high pitch of excitement, when he paused.

"I wish," he exclaimed, "that I had entire control of the Southern slaveholders for twenty-four hours."

A Southerner, seated at the back of the hall, jumped to his feet. "Mr. Chairman," he demanded, "may I ask the speaker one question?"

The chairman, anxious to avoid a row, replied in a conciliatory voice, "Mr. Henson has the platform, and no one must interrupt him without his permission."

At this point Josiah spoke up. "The gentleman at the back of the house may ask me the question," he said.

Well, just what would the Reverend Josiah Henson do with the slaveholders? the heckler sneered.

In the long silence that followed, Josiah's friends looked at him anxiously. What bitter thoughts of revenge were going through his mind? How would he respond?

"First," he said, speaking in a loud clear voice that showed no sign of agitation, "I would have them all converted to God."

Another pause. "Secondly, I would send them immediately to heaven—"

A gasp from the congregation, and then Josiah smiled.

"Before they had a minute's time to backslide," he finished.

The congregation rocked with laughter. Josiah felt heartened by the ovation when he sat down amid the cheers of his listeners.

After hearing Josiah Henson preach, Samuel Eliot suggested that he tell his life story for publication. Hundreds of such stories had appeared in abolitionist newspapers, and others were published in book or pamphlet form. Books by such black authors as Frederick Douglass and William Wells Brown were widely read. Theodore Weld, a leading white abolitionist, with the help of a staff of assistants, had combed Southern newspapers and the files of abolition societies to obtain the material for his book, *Slavery as It Is or Testimony of a Thousand Witnesses*. Accounts that gave former slaves a chance to speak for themselves went "right to the hearts of men," said one editor, and Eliot was convinced that the Henson story would furnish antislavery forces with another powerful argument.

Though Josiah was an able speaker, the mechanics of writing were difficult for a man who had not even learned to sign his name until he was in his forties. He therefore dictated his story during a number of visits to the Eliot home. By then Josiah was sixty years old. In thinking back over the years, he found it hard to remember all that had happened, and he forgot certain incidents that later he would recall under the prodding of a skillful editor. Josiah began his autobiography by telling about his birth in Maryland and ended with his move to Dawn in 1842. The final paragraph was a statement of his own high hopes:

> I will conclude my narrative by simply recording my gratitude to God and to many of my fellowmen; for the great degree of comfort with which I am surrounded; for the prospects opening to my children, so different from what they might have been; and finally for the cheering expectation of benefitting not only the present, but many future generations of my race.

When the manuscript was finished, Eliot paid to have it printed. On a later trip to Boston, Josiah visited the headquarters of the Massachusetts Anti-Slavery Society where his own slender volume of reminiscences was displayed alongside the more pretentious books by Frederick Douglass, William Wells Brown, and Theodore Weld.

The following year, 1850, another visitor came to the Massachusetts Anti-Slavery Society, a mere wisp of a woman, rather plain-looking at first glance, but with brooding dark eyes that made her face one to be remembered. She pored over several of the books on the library shelves. They had vigor. They rang true because they showed slave life as the slave himself saw it. One book that interested her especially was called *The Life of Josiah Henson, formerly a Slave.* It was only seventy-six pages long. She read it quickly, but she did not forget it.

Her name was Harriet Beecher Stowe.

14

⌒∾⌒

A Backward Glance—
Harriet in Cincinnati

Two years after the Hensons had escaped to Canada
by way of Cincinnati, several members of the
Beecher family had gone there to live. Dr. Lyman
Beecher, one of the country's leading clergymen, became president of Lane Seminary, a school recently
established to train preachers. Several Beecher sons
had entered the ministry or were preparing to. Catherine, the brilliant eldest daughter, was well known
as a home economist, author, and teacher. In Cincinnati, she hoped to start a pioneer college with the
help of her sisters, Mary and Harriet. Harriet, then a
young woman of twenty-one, helped in the school for
a while, but she was more interested in writing than
in teaching.

From a distance, Cincinnati was a picturesque
town set in an amphitheater of hills above the Ohio,
but Harriet never really liked it. The steamboats ply-
ing up and down the river helped to increase the
population from some thirty thousand people to several times that number during the eighteen years she
lived there. The "best people," proud of their

churches and schools and lighted streets, called their fast-growing city "the Athens of the West." But the boats also brought gamblers and other unsavory adventurers into the town. The chief cause of Harriet's distress, however, was her first closeup view of fellow human beings trying to escape from bondage.

After the Henson flight, more and more Negroes fled across the river from the slave state of Kentucky. When Harriet read advertisements in local newspapers about the large rewards offered for the capture of runaway slaves, she was sickened and shocked. She knew that her father abhorred the system yet did not see what could be done about it. Like many others, he was antagonized by Garrison's contention that, unless the slaves were freed at once, the North should secede from the Union.

"Were it in my power to put an end to slavery, I would do it, but it is not," said Dr. Beecher. He compared the abolitionists to men who "would burn down their houses to get rid of the rats."

At first Harriet was inclined to agree. Looking back years later, however, she said, "The results of time have shown that the young printer saw further than the sages of his day." The change in her thinking was gradual. She was deeply troubled by what was happening in Cincinnati. Her distress was even more intense after her marriage to Calvin Stowe, a professor at Lane. Like some of the other members of the faculty and many of the students, he was an ardent abolitionist, but, in the town, proslavery elements had gained the upper hand.

From their modest cottage in Walnut Hills, Calvin and Harriet Stowe watched riots in the streets below. They saw gangs of ruffians attack blacks, burn their

113

houses, and drag not only escaped slaves but also many free Negroes across the river to be sold into slavery. The more the abolitionists at Lane condemned such practices, the more the seminary felt threatened by proslavery mobs.

"Only the fact," said Harriet, "that the institution was two miles from the city, with a rough and muddy road up a long, high hill, proved its salvation. Cincinnati mud, known for its depth and tenacity, sometimes had its advantages."

As Harriet listened to stories by workers in the Underground Railroad, her heart was heavy. On several occasions runaway slaves found refuge in her home. A Negro woman who had been freed lived close by and sometimes helped out in the busy household.

"My cook, Eliza Buck," Mrs. Stowe wrote in a letter to a friend some years later, "had lived through the whole sad story of a Virginia-raised slave's life. She was raised in a good family as a nurse and seamstress. When the family became embarrassed financially, she was suddenly sold on to a plantation in Louisiana. She told me how, without any warning, she was suddenly forced into a carriage and saw her little mistress screaming and stretching her arms from a window toward her as she was driven away. She also told me of scenes on the Louisiana plantation when she lived there. At night she often left her cabin by stealth, ministering to poor slaves who had been mangled and lacerated by the lash.

"Then she was sold into Kentucky, and her last master was the father of all her children. On this point she maintained a delicacy and reserve that

114

seemed to me remarkable. She always called him her husband, and it was not till after she had been with me some years that I discovered the real nature of the connection. I shall never forget how sorry I felt for her, nor my feelings at her humble apology, 'You know, Mrs. Stowe, slave women cannot help themselves.' She had two very pretty quadroon daughters, with her hair and eyes, interesting children, whom I instructed in the family school with my own children."

Harriet felt special pity for families that had been broken up. When her own little son Charley died, her grief seemed more than she could bear. "I learned what a poor slave mother must feel when her child is torn away from her," she said. "In the depths of my sorrow, I felt that I could never be consoled, unless this crushing of my own heart might enable me to work out some great good for others."

It may have been at this time that the thought first occurred to Harriet of writing some sketches about slavery. Before she met Calvin she had written a geography for children. After her marriage she turned out a few articles and stories to supplement his meager income, and some of the stories were collected into a book entitled *The Mayflower.*

But nearly every year added a new baby to the family. Much as Harriet loved her children, they took her time and sapped her strength. She was devoted to Calvin, her learned husband, but he was absent-minded and impractical—a man who depended on his wife so completely it was like having another child to look after. Moreover, she considered writing about men and women in bondage almost too painful a subject. She expressed her frustration in a letter to Calvin while he was away seeking a better position in the East.

"Pray, what is there in Cincinnati to satisfy one whose mind is awakened on this subject?" she wrote. "No one can have the system of slavery brought before him without an irrepressible desire to *do* something, and what is there to be done?"

At that time the slavery situation seemed hopeless, as did her personal problems. Distressed by the condition of the slaves and grieving for her little son, she was too tired to try to earn even the pittance that her writing had brought. There never seemed to be enough money to meet expenses, and now she was pregnant again. Another baby to be provided for!

Then Calvin came home one bright spring day and brought good news. He was offered a position as a professor at Bowdoin College in Brunswick, Maine. First, though, he must complete his teaching duties at Lane and so could not leave for several months. Since the new baby would be born that summer, Harriet decided to go on ahead and get a new home ready in Brunswick. The two little children could stay with relatives in Cincinnati. She would take the three older ones with her.

It would not be an easy journey. In 1850, trains were slow and dirty, and she and the children would have to change trains in the middle of the night. In Pittsburgh they would board a canalboat. She looked forward to a brief visit in Brooklyn, New York, with her younger brother, Henry Ward Beecher, by now as famous a preacher as their father. After visits with other relatives in New England, she finally would reach Brunswick.

From the minute she made her decision, she had no chance to rest. Calvin was willing but no help at all as she packed. She made a list of the furniture he was to have shipped and bought the tickets. She was tired even before she started.

She felt exhilarated too. Now at last she could leave the distressing scenes in Cincinnati behind, and she resolved to stop worrying about slavery. There seemed to be no use, she admitted later, "to read or think or distress oneself about it."

This was a resolve she would find hard to keep.

15

❦

The Reverend Henson
Meets Mrs. Stowe

Harriet felt her spirits lift when she reached Brunswick. A cordial Bowdoin professor and his wife met her and insisted that she and the three children stay with them temporarily. They had rented a house for her—a plain solid kind of house, built along simple New England lines. When her furniture finally came, Harriet had to race against time to have everything in place before the new baby was born. It was a boy whom she named Charles after the first beloved little Charley who had died.

By September, Harriet had to admit that she was tired. She found someone to look after the children. Then she left for Boston for a much-needed rest. She looked forward to a tranquil visit with her brother, the Reverend Edward Beecher.

But there was little tranquillity in Boston. Here, as in Cincinnati, it was not possible to ignore the subject of slavery. Many people in New England, as throughout the North, seethed with indignation over a bill recently passed by the United States Congress. Some Southern leaders had threatened secession and talked openly about breaking up the Union. In an attempt to avoid the calamity of a civil war, Congress had decided on compromise—the Compromise of 1850—which, it was hoped, would satisfy both North and South.

One of the five provisions of the bill was a new Fugitive Slave Law. It was much stricter than an earlier law, which never had been rigidly enforced. The 1850 act gave federal agents the right to arrest a suspected fugitive in whatever state he might be found, even though he might have lived in freedom for years. It was a one-sided arrangement. An accused Negro had no recourse to law. A Southern master or his representative, by furnishing an affidavit claiming ownership, could demand in any court, even in the North, that a suspect be arrested and returned to slavery. Any citizen convicted of harboring a fugitive was subject to heavy fine and imprisonment.

The results were the opposite of what the lawmakers had anticipated when the new law was passed.

In Boston, hundreds of angry people attended a protest meeting in Faneuil Hall. Wendell Phillips, member of a prominent New England family who had given up a successful law practice to lecture against slavery, was the speaker. It was a base libel, he contended, to call the new act a constitutional law.

"We must trample it under our feet," he went on. "By peaceful resistance, we must say that the fugitive who has breathed Massachusetts air shall never go back. Many have been here from twelve to twenty years. Disobey this law until the courts rule it unconstitutional."

119

Prominent citizens and others not so prominent, including many once indifferent to slavery, refused to betray fellow human beings. They looked down on slave traders as low characters. That decent men and women were expected to cooperate with them was a shocking idea, and nowhere was there greater indignation than in the Beecher household.

Harriet was deeply stirred by the swift march of events. Nearly every day she heard stories of panic-stricken black families fleeing to Canada. Some of the fugitives, among the earlier arrivals in New England, now owned their own homes. They had good jobs, but everything had to be left behind in their anxiety to cross the border. The Boston Vigilante Committee was never more active and recruited many new members to protect the Negroes in their midst. When the mayor and alderman gave local police the power to arrest fugitives, the Committee issued a warning. In January 1851, signs posted throughout the city warned black people to be on the lookout for kidnappers, whoever they might be.

A few weeks earlier, at the height of the hysteria, Harriet Beecher Stowe had learned that Josiah Henson, whose book she had admired, was in Boston. According to the Fugitive Slave Law, he was still a fugitive. He ran the risk of arrest because he considered the trip necessary for business reasons. His generous and influential friends, Samuel Eliot, Amos Lawrence, and Dr. Henry Ingersoll Bowditch, who had financed the Dawn sawmill, had never pressured him, but he was nonetheless anxious to clear up his debt to them. With this in mind he had arranged for a schooner to deliver another load of black walnut to Boston. Optimistic as usual, he hoped that the lum-

CAUTION!!

COLORED PEOPLE

OF BOSTON, ONE & ALL,

You are hereby respectfully CAUTIONED and advised, to avoid conversing with the

Watchmen and Police Officers of Boston,

For since the recent ORDER OF THE MAYOR & ALDERMEN, they are empowered to act as

KIDNAPPERS

AND

Slave Catchers,

And they have already been actually employed in KIDNAPPING, CATCHING, AND KEEPING SLAVES. Therefore, if you value your LIBERTY, and the *Welfare of the Fugitives* among you, *Shun* them in every possible manner, as so many *HOUNDS* on the track of the most unfortunate of your race.

Keep a Sharp Look Out for KIDNAPPERS, and have TOP EYE open.

APRIL 24, 1851.

ber would bring a good price.

Josiah also brought with him several of his best specimens of walnut boards, which he planned to exhibit at the Great Exhibition soon to open in London, England. Boston friends gave him letters of introduction to prominent English antislavery leaders. In the midst of his preparations for his trip to England, Mrs. Stowe invited him to call on her at her brother's home.

Harriet once described herself as "about as thin and dry as a pinch of snuff; never much to look at in my best days and looking like a used-up article now." People who met her had a different impression.

"She is not a beautiful woman," said one acquaintance, "and yet her eyes are not often surpassed in beauty. They are dark and dreamy, and look as if some sorrowful scene haunted the brain."

Her face, however, seemed to glow as from some inward light when she talked with Josiah about his book. "She said she was glad it had been published," he later recalled, "and hoped it would open the eyes of the people to the enormity of the crime of holding men in bondage."

There was much else that Harriet wanted to know, so during the interview Josiah went into greater detail about some of the circumstances described in his autobiography and spoke of other events as well. It was easy to understand why he was a popular preacher. He made each incident he described so vivid that it stood out like a picture in Harriet's mind. She shuddered when he told about the vicious beating of his father. Little Si could not have been more than two or three, but his father's screams still echoed in his imagination.

Mrs. John C. Day

Harriet Beecher Stowe was 40
when she first met Josiah Henson

His childhood, though, had not been spent entirely in shadow. He also talked about the happier times when his family had belonged to Dr. McPherson—a period in his young life that came to an abrupt close when the doctor died. Harriet's face clouded again when he told how his brothers and sisters, one by one, were put on the auction block. He also mentioned the recent unsuccessful efforts of an Underground worker to rescue his brother Jacob.

The visitor seated across from Mrs. Stowe was not tall, but he had broad shoulders and a powerful physique. His heavy beard showed white against his dark skin. He had a noble face, she decided—the face of "a saintly man," but a saint who had come close to violence. She was deeply moved by his account of his journey down the Mississippi when, goaded almost beyond human endurance, he had considered murder to be his only hope for escape. Yet he had resisted the impulse. His eyes mirrored his distress as he recalled the experience.

When Harriet told him good-by, she little knew the consequences that their meeting was to have both for her and for her country.

Nor did Josiah Henson. He had his own personal problems. Due to a financial depression, the money received for his shipment of black walnut had fallen short of expectations. Again, his creditors were lenient and understanding. When he was able to offer them only part payment, one of the three, Samuel Eliot, gave a quarter of the money back. A short time later, when Josiah sailed for England, Eliot went down to the dock to wish him Godspeed. Quite a crowd had gathered, including several men who had contributed to a fund to make Josiah's trip possible.

They believed that he was embarking on a wise business venture. What was even more important, they were confident that in England he could accomplish much good for the antislavery cause.

As the American ship in which he was traveling plowed its slow way across the Atlantic, Josiah thought of the four walnut boards stowed away in the hold. At the Great Exhibition, he hoped they would bring enough orders for his lumber to wipe out the rest of his debts. Josiah was proud of those boards. He would plane them and polish them. He would make them shine like mirrors.

As a slave in Kentucky he had looked on the Ohio River and dreamed of what life would be like if only he could reach the farther shore. Now, with the wide waters of the ocean stretching in every direction, the horizon seemed without limit.

16

⚜

Exhibiting in
the Crystal Palace

The Crystal Palace was not like any building Josiah
Henson had ever seen. In that he was no different
from thousands of others who attended the Great
Exhibition during the fourteenth year of Queen Victoria's reign. Every day after the opening in the
spring of 1851, crowds milled around the "Glass Palace," a mammoth glass and iron structure in the
Hyde Park section of London.

"It was so graceful, so delicate, so airy," declared
one British statesman, "that its translucent beauty
remains graven on my memory. When I saw it glit-
tering in the morning sun, I felt as if Aladdin and the
genie who was the slave of the lamp must have been
at work on it—no mere human hands and hammers
and builders' tools could have wrought such a mira-
cle."

Certainly the Exhibition plans—which owed
much to Albert, the prince consort of the Queen—
were impressive. Victoria had invited the nations of
the world to send examples of their art and industry,

so they could "enter into amiable competition with each other."

When Josiah arrived, he found his walnut boards in the space set aside for the United States exhibit. He started to move them, when he was stopped by the superintendent of the American department, a man from Boston.

"Where are you taking those boards?" the American demanded.

"To the Canadian exhibit," Josiah replied.

"No, your lumber must stay where it is. You brought it over in an American ship, and it is a part of the American display. Not a single thing here must be moved an inch without my consent."

Josiah made no reply as he set to work to polish his walnut boards. But to himself he said, "All right, if this Yankee wants to exhibit my furniture, at least the world shall know who owns it." The next morning when the superintendent arrived, the boards were still in place. On top of them a sign had been painted, announcing in large letters:

This is the product of a Fugitive Slave from the United States, whose residence is Dawn, Canada.

"What under heaven have you got up there?" the superintendent demanded, pointing to the sign.

"Oh," said Josiah innocently, "that is just a little information to let people know who I am."

By this time a crowd had gathered, and everyone seemed to enjoy the situation, except the man from Boston. His face was flushed with anger.

"Do you suppose I'm going to let that insult stay?"

he asked. "Get your lumber out of here and take it wherever you please."

"I beg your pardon, sir," Josiah reminded him, "when I wanted to remove it you would not allow it. As you wanted it very much, I will not disturb it. You can have it now."

If the superintendent made any reply, it was lost in the laughter of the crowd. He was relieved when Josiah finally was "persuaded" to move his walnut boards to the section reserved for Canada.

Practically every nation in Europe, Asia, and the Americas was represented at the Great Exhibition. The products displayed were many and varied. The Koh-i-noor diamond, which translated meant "the mountain of light," was the largest diamond in the world. It came from the Punjab, a part of India, and attracted a constant stream of sightseers. A recent invention in the American section was just as popular but for a different reason. A group of British farmers usually was found gathered around a model of the McCormick reaper. This reaper, which was to bring about great changes in agriculture, was being shown in England for the first time.

The visitors at the Great Exhibition were as varied as the products they had come to see. British laborers and members of the nobility spent hours wandering among the stalls. Chinese gentlemen with hair hanging in braids down their backs mingled with tourists of a number of other nationalities. A few members of the African race were present, but Josiah was the only Negro exhibitor.

"Perhaps my complexion attracted attention," he said, "but nearly all who passed paused to look at me, and at themselves as reflected in my polished walnut

Josiah exhibited black walnut boards
from Dawn in the "Glass Palace"

boards. Among others, the queen of England, Victoria, preceded by her guide, paused to view me and my property."

"Is he indeed a fugitive slave?" she asked.

"He is indeed," the guide replied, "and that is his work."

The Queen was a homely little lady but cordial as she inclined her head in response to the Reverend Henson's respectful bow. Perhaps she had heard of him already as the eloquent Negro preacher from Canada. His letters from prominent antislavery leaders in America opened many doors, and he was invited to speak in several English churches.

The year before Josiah Henson went abroad, the trustees at Dawn had decided on a course of action that, it was hoped, would clear up some of their financial difficulties. Arrangements were made for the American Baptist Free Missions Society to take charge of the Institute. Josiah, with the help of another black resident, Peter B. Smith, agreed to be responsible for the mill. But to Josiah, who had been denied a formal education, the school was the project closest to his heart. His talks in England raised a considerable sum for the benefit of the British American Institute.

It was fashionable among some English aristocrats to welcome interesting and attractive fugitives. Most of them felt a genuine concern for those who had fled from bondage, and Josiah Henson was not the only Negro well known in Britain. During the past several years, Frederick Douglass, William Wells Brown, and other fugitives had lectured before large audiences throughout the British Isles, arousing sympathy for the antislavery cause.

The fugitives who attended the Great Exhibition shared in the general feeling of regret when the Crystal Palace closed its doors for the last time. Josiah Henson received a large quarto bound volume with a description of the various exhibits, with his own name recorded among the exhibitors. In addition he was awarded a bronze medal and was given a picture of the Queen and the royal family. These mementos would always serve as a reminder of the gratifying experience of a man, once considered a piece of property, who had won honor in freedom.

But the debts that he had assumed in Canada must still be paid. He was not yet ready to leave England.

17

❦

London—and a Changed America

The Great Exhibition closed in October 1851, but
Josiah stayed on in London to promote his lumber
business. He was in even greater demand as a
preacher, after a British edition of his book was published. English readers were much interested in the
American antislavery movement, many because
they disapproved of slavery.

Millowners and political leaders had an added reason. They feared that the growing hostility between
the United States North and South might bring about
a civil war that would threaten the way in which
many Englishmen made their living. One out of every eight persons in Britain worked in the cotton
mills, and the mills depended mostly on the American South for raw cotton. If war should come, it
seemed likely that Northern ships would try to block-
ade Southern ports, and cotton growers could not
then send their cotton abroad. It might be necessary
for British mills to develop new sources of supply.

One day Lord Henry George Grey, the home sec-
retary, made Josiah a surprising offer. He proposed

that Josiah go to India to superintend a British government project of cultivating cotton on the American plan. Obviously, Josiah lacked the experience needed for such a post. Cotton was not grown on the Maryland and Kentucky plantations where he had acted as overseer, but he was flattered by Lord Grey's offer. If at times he seemed unduly impressed by the attentions shown him by "fine gentlemen," he was guilty only of an all-too-human weakness. One of the high points of his stay in London was his interview with the Archbishop of Canterbury.

"Sir," the Archbishop asked Josiah, "at what university did you graduate?"

"I graduated from the school of adversity, your grace," Josiah replied. "It was my lot to be born a slave and to pass my first forty years in bondage. I never went to school, never read the Bible in my youth, and received all my training under the most adverse circumstances."

The Archbishop could not hide his astonishment. He seemed especially surprised by his guest's fluent use of English. Josiah explained that it had been his practice to listen carefully when educated people talked, and he had tried to imitate those who spoke correctly.

"I never would have suspected," the Archbishop said, "that you were not a liberally educated man."

Another memory that Josiah would always cherish was the day spent with a group of Sabbath-school teachers on the estate of Lord John Russell, the prime minister. Never had he seen such a magnificent park. Deer leaped unafraid across the lawns, and the trees seemed alive with the flutter of wings and the songs of birds. Dinner was served in the

133

spacious dining hall, and the Reverend Henson was seated at the head of the long table. At dinner he was asked to offer a toast. Though writing might be difficult for him, as a speaker he never seemed at a loss for words.

"First to England," he said, "honor to the brave, freedom to the slave. God bless the Queen."

He sat down amid cheers, but someone called, "Up, up again."

Since Josiah had found freedom in Victoria's dominion, he offered a special toast to her. "To our most Sovereign Lady, the Queen," he said. "May she reign in righteousness and rule in love."

Among the prominent Englishmen who entertained Josiah in their homes was Samuel Morley. Usually Josiah was a cheerful companion, but one day at dinner he seemed abstracted and depressed. He hardly touched his food.

"What's the matter, Josiah?" Samuel Morley asked.

"Please excuse me," was the halting reply. "I—I was thinking of my brother."

Not since he had learned that Jacob was alive had this brother been far from his thoughts. He told Mr. Morley about the Underground worker's failure to rescue Jacob. But surely, something could be done, Josiah added. Another effort must be made after he reached Canada.

By now he was planning his return. Through his lectures he had raised about a thousand pounds for the school at Dawn. This sum was turned over to the British and Foreign Anti-Slavery Society. The member of the group that Josiah most admired was John Scoble, a well-known antislavery leader. He had heard rumors that Scoble had enemies, but so did many other famous men. He was especially touched by Mr. Scoble's interest in the Institute. The man was a persuasive speaker, and members more experienced in the ways of the world than Josiah were impressed and deceived by his eloquence. Scoble convinced his London colleagues that the British American Institute could be made to thrive under proper management—in other words, under John Scoble's management.

The British Society, though it did not assume any financial responsibility, got in touch with the trustees at Dawn. The result was that Scoble was appointed resident superintendent of the Institute. He took charge of the money that Josiah had earned; it would help to pay the school's debts. Josiah was thrilled when Scoble, shortly before he left for Canada, outlined his plans. These included the construction of better school buildings and a model farm that would bring in a large annual income.

"I am going to renovate the place," he boasted.

"I shall never forget those words," Josiah said later. "They sounded so grand to my ears."

A short time afterward, a letter from his family in Canada drove all other thoughts from his mind. Charlotte, his wife for more than forty years, was dying, and he left at once for home. Charlotte's joy in seeing him revived the hope that she might still recover. This was not to be, but they had several weeks together.

"We talked over our whole past life," he wrote in his autobiography. "We reviewed scenes of sorrow and trouble, as well as the many bright and happy days, until she sank into a quiet sleep."

After Charlotte's death, Josiah was inconsolable,

135

but events would not permit a long period of mourning. Much had happened while he was away. The Underground Railroad had never done a more thriving business. After the passage of the Fugitive Slave Law thousands of new fugitives crossed the border into Canada. Josiah was still without a definite plan for rescuing his brother Jacob. His immediate task was to help care for the escapees who had found a temporary shelter at Dawn. He and the other older residents tried to find jobs and homes for the newcomers.

The sight of desperate men and women arriving day after day aroused many white Canadians to action. They joined the Anti-Slavery Society of Canada, recently organized by J. Brown, editor of the Toronto *Globe*.

"The question is often put: What have we in Canada to do with slavery?" he said at the first annual meeting. "We have everything to do with it. No man has the right to refuse his aid in ameliorating the woes of his fellowman. And there is another reason. We are in the habit of calling the people of the United States 'the Americans.' But we too are Americans. On us as well as on them lies the duty of preserving the honor of the continent."

Antislavery feeling in Canada undoubtedly had been strengthened by the Fugitive Slave Act. South of the Canadian border, those masters of propaganda, the abolitionists, used the unpopular law for their own advantage. Whenever a fugitive was dragged back to slavery in chains, his capture was publicized in antislavery newspapers to arouse the public to greater fury and resentment.

Nowhere was this more apparent than in Boston.

In 1850 Josiah Henson had run some risk when he insisted on staying in the city. When he visited there several years later, he was in no danger. Everyone seemed to be talking about slavery, but nothing was said in its defense. Instead, people were asking one another: What could be done about it? How could it be done away with?

The change in the people's thinking in Boston and throughout the North was due to the publication of a single book. It was called *Uncle Tom's Cabin; or Life Among the Lowly*, by Harriet Beecher Stowe.

Josiah thought for a minute. The name of the author had a familiar ring.

18

⌒⌒

The Miracle of
"Uncle Tom's Cabin"

The modest housewife whom Josiah Henson had met
before his departure for England was now the most
widely read author in the world. No one was more
surprised by her sudden fame than Harriet Beecher
Stowe herself. After her Boston visit in 1850, she had
returned to her home in Brunswick, Maine. She was
troubled by the callous indifference of many otherwise kind, good people, who seemed unaware of
what slavery was really like. Letters from her sister-
in-law, Mrs. Edward Beecher, were constant reminders of the "terrible things that were going on in Boston" as a result of the Fugitive Slave Law.

"What can I do?" one letter to Harriet read. "Not
much myself, but I know one who can. Hattie, if I
could use a pen as you can, I would write something
that would make this whole nation feel what an accursed thing slavery is."

Mrs. Stowe read this letter aloud to her children
assembled in her little parlor. Suddenly she rose,
crushing the letter in her hand.

"I *will* write something," she said, her lips set in

138

Stowe-Day Foundation

a determined line. "I will if I live."

She thought about it constantly. She wanted to picture scenes that would stir a reader, but the right ideas did not come. Perhaps she was too busy caring for her children, one of them a baby. Sometimes at night as she looked down at him sleeping beside her she broke into sobs. He made her think of the babies who were taken by force from their mothers. Those other babies were black. Their mothers were slaves.

Harriet's heart was "filled with anguish," as she wrote this same son years later, after he had grown to manhood, "excited by the cruelty and injustice our nation was showing to the slave."

Each Sunday she attended the little wooden church in Brunswick. One morning when she was seated in her pew a picture flashed into her mind— a picture so vivid it was like a vision. She seemed to see an aged slave being whipped to death. Perhaps, without realizing it, she remembered the brutal beating of Josiah Henson's father, as he had described it to her. She could not explain the "vision," but she was so deeply affected that she rushed home to put down on paper what she had seen, while it was fresh in her mind. She wrote rapidly, feverishly, and when she ran out of paper she used some brown wrapping paper to finish. When she read what she had written to her children, they burst into tears.

"Oh, Mama," said one of them, "slavery is the most cruel thing in the world."

After Calvin came home he read the same description. "This should be the climax of your story," he told her, the tears running down his cheeks. "Now write the chapters that lead up to it."

Encouraged by her husband's reaction, she sent a letter to the *National Era,* an antislavery newspaper in Washington. The editor had used some of her short sketches. Would he be interested, she asked, in a longer piece about slavery to publish as a serial? As soon as he replied, she set to work.

Her narrative would be told as fiction, she decided, but fiction based on fact. She remembered Josiah Henson's book. She recalled what he had told her in conversation, the experiences related by fugitive slaves in Cincinnati, and other accounts she had read in the antislavery press. In the beginning, she intended to have only a few chapters. But the story seemed to take possession of her, and she wrote on and on. To a person of her religious temperament, it seemed that "God wrote it," she declared later. She felt she was "only an instrument in his hands."

For forty weeks, chapter followed chapter, as Harriet struggled to meet the newspaper's weekly deadline. She wrote hastily, often not taking time to punctuate her copy or worry about correct grammatical construction.

But the story, deeply moving, had reality and suspense. One of the author's favorite characters was Eliza. The young slave mother, with a baby in her arms, fled across the half-frozen river from Kentucky, leaping from one cake of floating ice to another, with slave catchers in pursuit. After Eliza reached the Ohio shore, Underground workers cared for her until her husband, George Harris, also escaped and the reunited family finally reached Canada.

Chiefly, though, Mrs. Stowe's narrative was about Uncle Tom, a faithful slave. He reminded her of the Reverend Henson. As a boy, Josiah had had a kind master for a while. In Harriet's story Tom had a kind master who was forced to sell him in payment of a debt. On the boat carrying Tom to the slave market in New Orleans, Eva, the small daughter of Augustine St. Clair, fell overboard. Tom saved her from drowning, and, in gratitude, he was purchased by the child's father.

The little girl and the slave soon became good friends. In all fiction there probably never existed a more saintly child. After writing the scene describing Eva's death, Harriet was wrought up to such a high pitch of emotion that she had to take to her bed. In due time this emotion would be shared by thousands of readers, and they were equally affected when Uncle Tom had to be sold again.

This time the purchaser was the sadistic Simon Legree. Because Tom, a capable overseer, was too humane to enforce Legree's demands for harsh discipline against some of the other slaves, he suffered martyrdom. In the final scene—the one Harriet had created first and which showed slavery at its worst—Tom died as a result of a brutal beating. Nineteenth-century readers wept, and the labor of creation left Harriet exhausted.

"I write with my life's blood," she said.

She tried to lighten her narrative with humorous incidents. Comic relief was furnished by the character of Topsy, a mischievous black child who was the despair of St. Clair's cousin, Miss Ophelia, a prim maiden lady from Vermont. Harriet admitted that her story was an "inadequate representation of slavery."

"Slavery in some of its workings is too dreadful for purposes of art," she said. "A work that should represent it strictly as it is would be a work that could not be read."

One of her chief problems was that her only view of a slavery plantation was during a brief visit to Kentucky. She was entertained by a charming family whose slaves were treated kindly. She did not blame her hosts. It was the system that was at fault—a system that permitted one human being to own another. In writing, she depended on information that had been supplied by victims of that system and on her own imagination. She began her story while living in Brunswick. It was finished in Andover, Massachusetts, after Calvin became a professor at the theological seminary there. Before the final chapters appeared in the *National Era,* a Boston publisher, J. P. Jewett, offered Harriet a contract to publish her serial in book form.

She did not expect much of a sale; it simply was a story she felt she had to write. By the time she was through, she was so tired she wondered if anyone would want to read it. "I hope," she said plaintively, "that it will earn enough money for me to buy a new silk dress."

What then happened was one of the miracles of publishing. *Uncle Tom's Cabin; or Life Among the Lowly* came out in book form March 20, 1852, and sold three thousand copies the first day. It became a runaway best seller and seventeen printing presses were kept busy supplying the demand. In the days ahead, the book was translated into every known language. Because of defective copyright laws, the author received no payment on most of the foreign editions, but her first check from Mr. Jewett was for ten thousand dollars. She had enough to buy her new silk dress and a great deal more. For the first time in her married life, Harriet felt some measure of financial security.

What was more important to her was that her story pricked the conscience of the people. It did more to awaken them to the evils of the slave system than the abolitionists had been able to do in hundreds of articles and speeches. Readers who seldom listened to a political speech began to demand freedom for the slave.

Harriet also was pleased by the reaction of other authors. Elizabeth Barrett Browning, the English poet, was touched, in spite of what she called "the wretched writing." Many famous writers praised her without any reservation at all. John Greenleaf Whittier, the Quaker poet, said he gave thanks for the Fugitive Slave Law, since "it gave occasion to *Uncle Tom's Cabin.*" Jenny Lind, the Swedish prima donna who was on a concert tour in America, sent the author a fan letter. "I have the feeling about *Uncle Tom's Cabin,*" Jenny wrote, "that great changes will take place by and by."

These changes were what Harriet, in her modest way, had hoped for. She also was heartened by hundreds of other letters from persons of whom she had never heard. The characters in her book were composites, but they seemed so real that some of the letter writers were convinced they had known the men and women she described. A number of exciting escapes similar to that of Eliza had been reported in the abolitionist press. Several readers remembered children like Topsy. Others, including Harriet's brother Charles while visiting New Orleans, had met sadists like Simon Legree. Harriet's view was that he was representative of many men, not only on plantations, but in London, New York, and New England. Given the opportunity, they would be just as cruel.

"The only difference is that," she said, "in free states, Legree is restrained by law; in the slave states, the law makes him an absolute, irresponsible despot."

Strangest of all was the fact that many of the readers who had wept over Uncle Tom's tragic death claimed to have known him "in such and such a state." Obviously, there were more slaves like Uncle Tom than most Americans had realized, and Harriet's portrayal was not intended as the biography of

144

135,000 SETS, 270,000 VOLUMES SOLD.

UNCLE TOM'S CABIN

FOR SALE HERE.

AN EDITION FOR THE MILLION, COMPLETE IN 1 Vol., PRICE 37 1-2 CENTS.

" " IN GERMAN, IN 1 Vol., PRICE 50 CENTS.

" " IN 2 Vols., CLOTH, 6 PLATES, PRICE $1.50.

SUPERB ILLUSTRATED EDITION, IN 1 Vol., WITH 153 ENGRAVINGS,

PRICES FROM $2.50 TO $5.00.

The Greatest Book of the Age.

any one man. She gave chief credit, however, to Josiah Henson, now in his early sixties and very much alive.

"His real history," said Harriet, "in some points goes beyond that of Uncle Tom in his heroic manhood."

Uncle Tom's Cabin proved to be a "natural" for the stage, but it was dramatized without the author's consent. At that time, there were no copyright laws to protect her dramatic rights, and the "Tom shows" distorted the book. Playwrights in a number of different versions of the play did whatever they pleased with her material. They added or enlarged sensational scenes. Actors who took the lead often played the part for laughs, changing Uncle Tom into a fawning, ridiculous flunky. The character, as they portrayed him, bore little resemblance to the Reverend Josiah Henson.

Not all of Harriet's mail praised her. She had been naïve enough to hope that her book might help to heal the widening breach between the two sections of the country. She considered slavery not a sectional but a national problem. Northerners who profited from the manufacture and sale of cotton goods, as well as shipowners who transported raw cotton for use in British cotton mills, must accept their share of the blame.

The author also tried to understand the dilemma of many Southerners, enmeshed in a system they had inherited. She had liked and admired her Kentucky hosts and other Southerners she knew personally. For a brief period during his childhood, Josiah Henson had a kind master, and in her book Harriet

146

showed masters who were humane as well as those who were cruel.

Having leaned over backward in her effort to be fair, she was shocked when the hate letters began pouring in. Her book was not permitted to be sold in many Southern towns and had to be read surreptitiously if at all. One day she received a package containing a black human ear. She could only hope that it had been cut from a corpse, but she remembered the experience of the young Josiah's father.

What bothered Harriet's New England conscience were accusations that her descriptions of slavery were exaggerated. Since her book took the form of fiction, she did not need to defend it, but this she was determined to do.

"I am now very much driven," she wrote to a friend toward the end of 1852. "I am preparing a 'Key' to unlock *Uncle Tom's Cabin*. It will contain all the original facts, anecdotes, and documents on which the story is founded, with some interesting and affecting stories parallel to those told of Uncle Tom."

The second part of this statement was more accurate than the first. While she was working on the "Key," Calvin located newspaper articles, books, and documents of which his wife had not known while writing *Uncle Tom's Cabin*. Yet this new material justified scenes that had been the product of her imagination. Descriptions of new incidents that her husband discovered were often similar to those described by Josiah Henson and others whose stories Harriet had read.

The *Key* was finished in April 1853. Harriet, Calvin, and her brother Charles Beecher then left for England and Scotland, where they were the guests of British antislavery societies. At the pier in Liverpool a crowd waited to welcome her. The slight little woman in the plain high-necked dress, her eyes bright under her poke bonnet, was embarrassed to be the object of so much attention.

"It seems to me so odd and dreamlike," she wrote home to her children, "that so many persons desire to see me."

Newspapers announced her comings and goings. *Punch*, the English weekly, published an amusing picture of John Bull with an open copy of her book, weeping over "the sorrows of poor Uncle Tom."

In Scotland, Harriet received the same cordial welcome. Receptions were held in her honor, and gifts of money were pressed on her. She was especially touched by a national penny offering, small coins collected by committees from the poor in Edinburgh and Glasgow who wanted to help the kind of people of whom Mrs. Stowe had written.

After her return home, Harriet saw the Reverend Henson again. In their later years, both of them were hazy about dates, but both remembered a meeting in Harriet's home in Andover. By then Josiah had read *Uncle Tom's Cabin* and the *Key*, or, more likely, one of his sons or daughters had read the books to him. In her *Key*, Harriet acknowledged her debt to the little volume published in 1849, in which Josiah told his life story up until that time.

"If my humble words in any way inspired that gifted lady to write such a plaintive story that the whole community has been touched with pity for the sufferings of the poor slave, I have not lived in vain,"

"John Bull, Lamenting the Sorrows of Poor Uncle Tom," in the famous British magazine, *Punch*

he said. "Though she made her hero die, it was fit that she did this to complete her story. If God had not given to me a giant's strength, I should have died over and over again long before I reached Canada. I regard it as one of the most remarkable features of my life that I have rallied after so many exposures to all kinds of hardships."

The Reverend Henson, like a number of Harriet's correspondents, was convinced that he had known the originals of some of her other characters. He had told her about his friends, Lewis Clark, the prototype of George Harris, and Eliza, George's wife. Chloe, the cook in the big house, reminded him of his late wife, Charlotte. Topsy was very much like Dinah, the mischievous child he had known during his plantation days. The kind master, whom Harriet called Augustine St. Clair in her story, was like Josiah's old neighbor, St. Clair Young. Susan, his daughter, whom Josiah had once saved from drowning, might have been little Eva. Like Mrs. Stowe's brother, Josiah felt sure that he had known the real Simon Legree. The man Charles Beecher met lived in New Orleans. The one Josiah remembered was from Maryland.

"Bryce Litton, who broke my arms and maimed me for life," Josiah said, "would stand very well for Mrs. Stowe's cruel Legree. Litton was the most tyrannical, barbarous man I ever saw. Mrs. Stowe's book is not an exaggerated account of the evils of slavery. The truth has never been half told; the story would be too horrible to hear."

It may have been during his visit to Andover that Josiah confided to Mrs. Stowe some recent news he had received about his brother Jacob. Through anti-slavery friends he had learned that Jacob's owners, now living in Maryland, were willing to sell him. In order to raise the sum asked and to pay for his transportation, Josiah needed five hundred and fifty dollars. He believed that he could earn this sum by updating his book and including chapters about his remarkable experiences in England. It was to be called, appropriately enough, *Truth Stranger Than Fiction*. Amos Lawrence agreed to finance its publication, and Mrs. Stowe wrote the following introduction:

> The numerous friends of the author of this little work will need no greater recommendation than his name to make it welcome. Among all the interesting records to which the institution of American slavery has given rise, we know of none more characteristic than that of Josiah Henson. Our excellent friend has prepared this edition of his work for the purpose of redeeming from slavery a beloved brother.

When the new books came off the press in 1858, Josiah carried a pack on his back and traveled through New England, offering copies for sale. The venture was successful, and he earned enough money to buy his brother's liberty. A cashier in a Boston bank sent the money to friends in Baltimore. They saw to it that Jacob had his freedom papers and arranged for his passage on a boat leaving for Boston.

The two former slaves who had not seen each other since childhood had a joyful reunion on the dock. Then Josiah took his brother home with him to Canada, where he was to live, a free man, for the next fifteen years.

19

⤳⤳⤳

A Time of Happiness;
A Time of Crisis

Harriet Beecher Stowe was indebted to Josiah Henson, and he was indebted to her. Some of her fame rubbed off on him, and he was in even greater demand as a speaker among antislavery groups in New England. He became more and more identified with the character of "Uncle Tom," though he himself never made that claim. He did not need to. Mrs Stowe had done that in her *Key*. In Boston and other towns, he found many reminders of *Uncle Tom's Cabin* in pictures, statues, and various souvenirs portraying Eva, Topsy, and other characters in the story. One well-known artist had made a life-size colored engraving of Uncle Tom himself.

In contrast to Mrs. Stowe's martyred hero, Josiah Henson at sixty-nine was as "blithe and active as a youth of sixteen," according to Henry Bleby, a Boston acquaintance. The Reverend Henson, said Mr. Bleby, was of "middle size, firm and well knit, clothed in a new glossy suit of clerical broadcloth.

"He was all over black," the description continued, "except his sparkling cravat and a set of

Artists and souvenir makers filled the
markets with "Uncle Tom" mementos

pearly white teeth. Again and again did laughter spread over his countenance and tell of a rollicking, fun-loving spirit that could not often be clouded with gloom. On looking at him more closely as he stood before me, holding a glossy white beaver hat in one hand while he extended the other in friendly salutation, I observed that both his arms were crippled, so that he could by no means use them freely. I shall not readily forget the rollicking enjoyment with which he related to me some of the experiences of his Canadian life. He was always looking on the bright side of things."

After four lonely years without Charlotte, Josiah had married again. Nancy, a widow he had met in Boston, had been brought up in Baltimore in a Quaker household where she had received a fair education. Both of her parents had once been slaves. But her mother, a superior laundress, had earned enough money to buy freedom both for herself and for her husband.

"Nancy has made me an excellent wife," Josiah was to say years later, "and my cup has indeed run over with God's mercies."

The year of Josiah's second marriage, 1858, was a time of crisis for the United States. Antislavery sentiment was growing in the North, and the activities and accusations of abolitionists aroused increasing anger in the South. A civil war, which the Fugitive Slave Law had been intended to avert, now seemed inevitable due to a recent decision of the United States Supreme Court. Dred Scott, a Negro belonging to a white man in the slave state of Missouri, had been taken by his master to the free territory of Minnesota. On their return to Missouri, the black man claimed that, because he had lived in free territory for several years, he was now free.

The case finally reached the United States Supreme Court, but went against Dred Scott. The decision, as rendered by Chief Justice Roger B. Taney, was that slaves were not citizens but the property of their owners, and the Constitution granted Congress no power over private property.

As for the words "All men are created equal" in the Declaration of Independence, the Chief Justice had this to say: "It is too clear for dispute that the enslaved African race were not intended to be included."

These words enraged and saddened leaders, both black and white, in the antislavery movement. The Supreme Court decision was the subject of a heated debate in August 1858 at a convention of Massachusetts Negroes in New Bedford. The Reverend Henson was among those seated on the platform when Charles L. Redmond, a fiery black orator, rose to speak. The time had come, said Redmond, for Negroes to take matters into their own hands, with bowie knife, revolver, and musket. He moved that a committee be appointed to prepare an appeal to the slaves of the South to rise in revolt.

According to a story published a few days later in *The Liberator*, an abolitionist newspaper, Redmond "doubted if his motion could be carried." But he didn't want to "see people shake their heads, as he did see them on the platform, and turn pale, but to rise and talk."

The Reverend Henson took up the challenge. As

155

for turning pale, he said with a smile, his teeth showing white in a very black face, he had never turned pale in his life.

His next words were more serious. Certainly he believed in Redmond's goals but not in his methods. Redmond might talk and run away, but what about the other poor fellows who must stay? The slaves had few weapons, and several thousand black men probably would be hanged. Then how could word of an impending uprising be circulated among them?

"Catch the masters permitting that," Josiah continued, "and you catch a weasel asleep. When I fight, I want to whip somebody."

The Reverend Henson's pragmatic view of the situation prevailed, and Redmond's motion was voted down. The following year another hotheaded abolitionist, this time a white man named John Brown with shaggy whiskers and piercing eyes, plotted a similar uprising. He managed to raise a small force to raid the United States Government arsenal at Harpers Ferry, then a part of Virginia. His plan was to seize the guns and ammunition needed to arm a massive rebellion of slaves throughout the South. Instead, he and his handful of followers were soon taken captive by a force of United States Marines. Two of Brown's sons were killed, and he was wounded. On the day of his trial he lay on a cot, still too weak to stand and looking much older than his fifty-nine years.

"I am yet too young," he said, "to understand that God is any respecter of persons. I believe that to interfere as I have done—as I have always freely admitted I have done—in behalf of his despised poor, was not wrong but right. Now if it is deemed necessary that I should forfeit my life for the furtherance of the ends of justice and mingle my blood . . . with the blood of millions in this slave country whose rights are disregarded by wicked, cruel, and unjust enactments—I submit; so let it be done."

Not since the publication of *Uncle Tom's Cabin* had Northerners and many Canadians who read accounts of the trial been so deeply stirred. Brown was condemned to hang as a traitor, but his was a glorious failure.

"You may dispose of me very easily," he said a month later on the way to the scaffold. "I am nearly disposed of now; but this question is still to be settled —the Negro question I mean; the end of that is not yet."

Events proved him right, for the threat of civil war hung heavy over the United States. Soon after his death, hundreds of people opposed to slavery were singing the words:

John Brown's body lies amould'ring in the grave . . .
His soul goes marching on!

During this same period Josiah Henson, in spite of his happiness with Nancy, had difficult personal problems. When he came home from England, he found that Peter Smith, who had been left in charge of the sawmill, had disappeared. Before he left, Smith had ordered three vessels loaded with sawed lumber but promised to return soon with supplies needed for the mill. After a while, his workmen, more than forty of them, realized he did not intend to come back. No one knew where he had gone, and he owed them several weeks' wages. They took out their anger on the mill, tearing down the valuable building. Not even the foundations were left standing.

"With the mill gone," said Josiah Henson, "I felt as if I had parted with an old friend."

Now he would not be able to fill orders he had received in England for lumber. Another disappointment was his loss of faith in John Scoble. In England, Josiah had almost venerated the well-known antislavery leader. The residents at Dawn, however, found him pompous and overbearing. They reported that their superintendent had taken possession of the entire farm belonging to the Institute. Any profits, they were convinced, went into his own pockets. Though Scoble had little practical knowledge of farming, he bought expensive farm machinery. He bought cattle without considering how they could be fed during the cold winter months. Debt was piled on debt.

As for the school, the building was so run-down that it could not be used. Several years had passed since Scoble promised new and better buildings, but they had not even been started. Josiah was troubled especially by the lack of a school—the school he had counted on to help the members of his race.

At first John Scoble refused to discuss the matter, but Josiah persisted. "The people here," he said, "are beginning to talk very hard about you and myself. I can satisfy them if only you will give me some idea when you intend to commence the new school buildings."

"When I get ready," was the curt reply.

"The people are growling."

"Let them growl."

"It is unfortunate for me," Josiah reminded him,

Dresden, Ontario

Henson's second wife, Nancy,
stood by him through financial difficulties

"as I have always defended you. My honor is impeached."

"What's your honor to me? I did not come here for colored people to dictate to me."

"If you do not intend to build us a school," said Josiah firmly, "you ought to leave the farm and let us manage for ourselves."

Scoble's face was red with anger. "Pay me what I have expended during the years I have tried to make this place meet its expenses, and I will go at once," he said.

The decision of what to do next had to be made by Josiah Henson. Hiram Wilson, whose advice he valued, had been living in the town of St. Catherine's for several years. The trustees could not be counted on for much help. They seemed to have lost interest in the Institute, so Henson called a convention of the black people in the community.

"I admit," he told them sadly, "I was deceived in Mr. Scoble. I had great faith in his integrity and believed every word he uttered. As the land was in splendid condition, he probably wanted to have a model farm that would bring in a regular income. He may have intended, as he promised, to have a splendid school which would be the pride of the neighborhood. If he had been a practical farmer, he doubtless could have accomplished those blessed results. But you know what happened. Year after year has passed, and there is still no school. Mr. Scoble has supported his family from the farm that belonged to us colored people. Yet he has no title to the land and no right to do this. Now if we are ever to have a school again—"

He paused, and someone in the audience spoke

up. "What *can* we do, Reverend?"

"We must gain possession of our property again."

"But how?"

"If you will give me the authority, I'll ask for legal advice."

The men at the meeting voted that the Reverend Henson should go ahead and consult lawyers. Scoble also hired a lawyer, and a series of lawsuits began. To meet expenses, Josiah mortgaged the farm he had acquired after much effort and frugality.

When or how the lawsuits would be decided, no one knew in 1860 when Abraham Lincoln was elected President of the United States. Quarrels between the Northern and Southern states—especially quarrels about slavery—had grown more bitter with each passing year. Because Lincoln had opposed the extension of slavery into western territory that was still free, many Southerners feared that his election was a threat to their interests. Even before his inauguration, seven Southern states (to be joined later by four others) seceded from the Union and set up a government for a separate nation called the Confederate States of America.

In his Inaugural Address the President assured Southerners he did not intend to interfere with slavery where it already existed. He had no constitutional authority to do so in time of peace. He also reminded them that no state had a legal right to secede from the Union; that in a democracy the minority must abide by the will of the majority of voters. Most Southerners believed that the federal, or national, government had no authority to overrule a decision voted by a state government. The Confederacy began to raise an army to defend what they

161

considered the rights of Southern States.

In April 1861 when Confederate troops bombarded Fort Sumter, a United States fort in the harbor of Charleston, South Carolina, President Lincoln called for federal volunteers to put down what most Northerners considered an insurrection. The American Civil War, which began with the bombardment of Fort Sumter, was to go on for four agonizing years.

In the beginning, Abraham Lincoln said that the purpose of the war was to preserve the Union. Canadians were interested only in the slavery problem. Later, to help win the war, the President issued the Emancipation Proclamation as a military measure. It announced that slaves should be "thenceforward and forever free" in all states or parts of states still in rebellion against the Federal Government on New Year's Day, 1863. The order could apply only to territory conquered by Union armies, but Northern victories finally assured all black Americans of liberty. Meanwhile, the Emancipation Proclamation made the American President a hero, loved and revered by thousands of Canadians. There was a great outpouring of grief when, five days after the end of the war, he was assassinated.

"Almost all of us," wrote the editor of the Toronto *Globe*, "feel as if we had suffered a personal loss."

For the Henson family, there was an added sorrow. Tom, who as a twelve-year-old boy had taught his father to read, enlisted on an American warship as soon as Negroes were permitted to join the Union forces. Josiah's firstborn, who would always hold a special place in his heart, was never heard from again. Presumably he had been lost at sea.

The crisis at Dawn, however, left little time for personal grief. The war between Henson and Scoble continued.

20

⟨❦⟩

Still Young in Spirit

During the next seven years, Josiah Henson sued John Scoble, and Scoble sued Henson. Scoble was never legally convicted of fraud, but seems to have acted through self-interest and was forced to resign. Henson had made mistakes, but they were mistakes of judgment, not of intent, and he had the interests of his people at heart. Money earned from his lectures and books had gone to help the fugitives, and his property was mortgaged to pay lawyers.

Now that American slaves were free, the security offered by Dawn and several other Negro communities was no longer needed. Many of the Negroes, shivering during the Canadian winters and homesick for relatives left behind, returned to the United States.

Finally the Court of Chancery appointed a new board of trustees for the Dawn Institute. The new board decided to sell the rich acres of land belonging to the school and nearly thirty thousand dollars was realized from the sale. After the debts of the Institute were paid, the rest of the money was used to establish

Uncle Tom's Cabin Museum

Through boom times and bad, Josiah lived in the
two-story frame cottage he had built at Dawn

a school at Chatham. It was called the Wilberforce
Educational Institute, in memory of William Wilberforce, the early English abolitionist. For a number of
years it continued to serve black students.

After his resignation, John Scoble returned to England, but Josiah continued to live in the two-story
frame cottage he had built for his family. He had
plenty of time to ponder over what had gone wrong.
To try to establish a school and a town in the wilderness, with the aid of inexperienced fugitives, was a
task few men would have attempted. Much of his
time and that of Hiram Wilson had been spent away
from Dawn raising money. The settlers—like anti-

slavery groups in the United States and like some of the different religious denominations that tried to help—had been divided by feuds among themselves.

The Reverend Henson, a man of strong convictions, was revered by many, but others accused him of mismanagement. He blamed himself for his early support of John Scoble, but, with his wry sense of humor, it rather pleased him to remember a heated argument with Scoble's son.

As Josiah Henson told the story, he had leased a plot of ground on the school farm while Scoble was still serving as superintendent. Several men working for Henson were plowing when young Scoble appeared and ordered them to leave.

"I leased this land from your father," Josiah told him, "I have the legal right to work this plot, and I shall defend that right."

"Why, Mr. Henson," the young man taunted him, "I thought you were a praying man, not a fighting man."

"When it is necessary I can fight. I intend to respect the rights of others, and they must respect mine."

When young Scoble became angry, words were followed by blows.

"I could not prevent him from bruising his head several times against my heavy walking stick," Josiah recalled, "which I held before me to ward off the blows he attempted to level at me."

Threatened with arrest, Josiah harnessed his horse, climbed into his wagon, and rode off in a hurry. He returned with a constable and had his assailant arrested instead. This was one of several times when he took up legal cudgels in his own defense, the kind of defense that would have been denied the hero in Harriet Beecher Stowe's story. The Reverend Henson considered himself as deeply religious as Uncle Tom, but he never permitted an unjust accusation to go unchallenged. He had accomplished too much under trying circumstances to bow gracefully to criticism. Uncle Tom would not have laughed over the encounter with John Scoble's son. Josiah Henson did.

The term "slave psychology" would have sounded strange in his ears. He only knew that he had overcome the limitations imposed by the slavery system. This was also true of many other fugitives. As a Methodist preacher, Josiah had traveled over a district of three hundred miles, held meetings, and established churches. In some of the homes he visited, he found books and newspapers read by people who a few years before had not known one letter from another. Many owned their own homes and had bought farms. Certainly much good had been accomplished.

Yet the special project to which the Reverend Henson had devoted more than thirty years was apparently a failure. The only reminder of the school with the impressive name—the British American Institute—was a dilapidated two-story building with broken windows. What was left of Dawn was now a part of the town of Dresden.

A man less optimistic might have been crushed by disappointment, but Josiah found reasons to be grateful. Dawn had been there when it was most needed. It had provided shelter for escaped slaves, a chance for them to earn a living, and a school where both children and adults could get an education. Unlettered though he was, Josiah Henson was a pioneer in promoting a school where students could work part-time and workers could study part-time. Years later a similar idea would be adopted by such American institutions as Tuskegee Institute and Berea College.

Most of all, perhaps, Josiah liked to recall the slaves he had helped to free. How happy his mother would have been to know that he and at least one brother, Jacob, had been reunited. After slavery was abolished in the United States, Jacob's son came for his father. The son now had a good position as superintendent of a dairy farm in New Jersey, and he wanted to take his father home with him.

"The meeting would have done President Lincoln's heart good if he could have witnessed it," Josiah said.

He was proud of his own family. Isaac, who had escaped with his parents to Canada, had been ordained as a minister, much beloved when he died at the age of thirty-seven. The younger Josiah attended college in Adrian, Michigan, then went into business and prospered. Peter, Charlotte's youngest son, stayed at home to look after the farm. Four daughters, born to Nancy, received the education that had been denied their father. One of them attended Oberlin College in Ohio. All were now married, and Josiah had the cherished companionship of grandchildren.

"He had a very jolly laugh," John Harris, a white neighbor, remembered. "He shook all over when he felt amused, which was often. The boys used to tease him to hear him laugh. In June he'd say, 'Come on, chilluns, strawberries is ripe!' and you couldn't see the ground for children rushing for strawberries and cream."

The children never guessed that their grandfather

was worried about the mortgage on his property or the debts he owed. Some of his friends knew and tried to find ways to help him. One of them, another minister, wrote to Harriet Beecher Stowe. In reply, he received a letter from her dated May 31, 1876, in which she wrote:

"I take pleasure in endorsing with all my heart that noble man, Josiah Henson, to be worthy of all the aid and help which any good man may be disposed to give. It is also true that a sketch of his life, published many years ago by the Anti-Slavery Society of Massachusetts, furnished me with many of the finest conceptions and incidents of Uncle Tom's character, in particular the scene in which he refuses to free himself by the murder of a brutal master . . . , and personal conversation confirmed my high esteem I had for him. I heartily hope he may have friends to assist him in his difficulties."

Another clergyman, a missionary of the Church of England, living in Dresden, suggested that the Reverend Henson go back to England. Perhaps some of the friends he had made there would remember him and rally to his assistance. Because of this clergyman's influence, Josiah soon received an invitation to visit the country where he had made his reputation as an orator twenty-five years earlier.

To a man still young in spirit at the age of eighty-seven, the visit was a thrilling prospect. Before he sailed, several prominent Canadians gave him letters of introduction to friends across the water. One letter read:

"Josiah Henson (Mrs. Stowe's Uncle Tom) proposes

starting in a week or two for England. His principal object will be to try to raise money to clear off a heavy mortgage he had to give on his farm in order to meet the cost of a long lawsuit over the Dawn Institute property, and which but for him would have been entirely lost. Mr. Henson bore the whole expense of that suit, and when the case was settled it was found that the trustees, appointed by the Court of Chancery, had no power to refund him out of the estate. The proceeds of the sale of the Dawn property, nearly thirty thousand dollars, constitute the greater part of the endowment of the Wilberforce Educational Institute. You will be pleased to learn that this institute is now in active operation, and if only wisely managed will be a great blessing . . . to the colored people of Canada.

"A voyage to England is no light undertaking for a man of Henson's extreme age. Yet he still possesses extraordinary energy both of body and mind. Knowing as I do his circumstances, and the hardship of his case, I sincerely hope he may be successful."

Several other letters written in Josiah Henson's behalf mentioned his connection with Mrs. Stowe's novel. His spirits lifted. In his speeches he had never identified himself with the character of Uncle Tom. But he could not help being pleased when others did.

21

❦

"Uncle Tom" in Britain

When Josiah reached England, accompanied by his wife, he found several old friends still living. They welcomed him not only as the Reverend Henson but also as "Uncle Tom." These friends, who included Samuel Morley, now a member of Parliament, started a fund to send him back to his Canadian home "with a light heart."

"I am certain," Josiah said, "that my heart will be heavy with gratitude."

He also made new friends, among them "Professor" Lorenzo Fowler, the phrenologist, who had recently moved to London from New York. The so-called science of phrenology, then very popular in both cities, was based on the assumption that character traits and ability could be determined by examining the formation of the skull— "the bumps on the head," as the saying went.

"I told him," Josiah recalled, "I should have supposed my old master had beaten out all my brains, but he humorously remarked that perhaps my skull was so thick, the blows did not penetrate."

Fowler's analysis of Josiah Henson was based in part on personal observation and knowledge of the former slave's past activities. When it was published in *The Christian Age,* a weekly magazine with a normal circulation of eighty thousand, the article aroused so much interest that second and third editions of the magazine had to be printed to meet the demand. Since then, phrenology has been discredited as a science, but the article portrayed Josiah Henson as he appeared to many Britons in 1877. Professor Fowler wrote:

> His head is narrow, long and high. The strength of his *social* nature centers in love for his wife and children, especially the latter, which was proved to be intense, by carrying two of his children on his back six hundred miles while fleeing from slavery and seeking freedom in Canada. He has a vast amount of dry humor and is very direct, practical, natural, and truthful in his style of talking. Though in his eighty-eighth year, he appears to be at least fifteen years younger, for he is firm in step, erect in form, and still anxious to make improvements.
>
> I am much gratified in making the acquaintance of "Uncle Tom," and hope that the friends of the colored race in England will send him back to Canada with sufficient means to enable him to live in comfort the remainder of his days.

Another new friend was John Lobb, managing editor of *The Christian Age.* Young Lobb, both a minister and an astute businessman, offered to arrange speaking engagements for the Reverend Henson. Moreover, since more than twenty years had passed since the publication of *Truth Stranger Than Fiction,* he suggested that the book be brought up to date,

Even in his eighties, Henson was sturdy and handsome

and he was listed on the title page as the editor. In gratitude, Josiah turned over the copyright to him and, though Josiah made very little money out of the book, John Lobb made a great deal. Lobb was a skillful interviewer. Under his probing questions, Josiah recalled many details not mentioned in his earlier books.

The new book retained the preface Mrs. Stowe had written for the 1858 edition, as well as introductory notes by Lobb, Samuel Morley, Wendell Phillips, and John Greenleaf Whittier among others. Also, on the title page, the Reverend Josiah Henson was identified as "Uncle Tom," which whetted the appetite of the British public to hear him speak.

The schedule of Josiah Henson during the months he spent in England and Scotland would have exhausted many a younger man. He spoke no fewer than ninety-nine times, telling overflow audiences the story of his escape from slavery. Frequently, an audience would join him in singing Negro songs, and collections were taken for the "Mr. Henson fund." Nancy sometimes sat on the platform while her husband spoke, and gifts were pressed on both of them. One present that pleased them especially was a music box to be taken home to their grandchildren.

After their visit in one town, the Hensons went on a tour of the surrounding countryside. Their host pointed out to them a certain tall tree and under it a stone bench that had been placed there as a memorial to William Wilberforce, one of England's pioneer antislavery leaders.

"Here was where it really began," the host explained. "William Wilberforce was a young man when he was elected to the House of Commons. One day soon after his election, he stood under this same tree with his friend, William Pitt, the prime minister. He told the Prime Minister that he was resolved to introduce a motion in Commons that the slave trade be abolished. Eight years went by before the measure was passed. Then Wilberforce worked for twenty-six more years for the passage of another bill that set all slaves free in lands under British rule."

Josiah beckoned to Nancy, and she sat down beside him on the memorial bench. They looked up at the historic tree. The school at Dawn was no more, but it was good to know that the sale of the property would benefit the Wilberforce Institute in Chatham.

"Our years of work were not wasted," said Josiah softly. "I am glad that the new school is named for such a great man."

In early March the Hensons went to Windsor Castle. Queen Victoria, still in mourning for her beloved Albert, the prince consort, received few visitors except relatives and those who had public business to transact. Yet when John Lobb sent her a copy of Josiah's book and informed her that "Uncle Tom" was in London, the name seemed to work a special magic. Lobb was invited to bring Mr. and Mrs. Henson to call at Windsor Castle.

On the train going down to Windsor, Josiah felt both honored and anxious. He remembered Victoria as a queen still in her early thirties, who had paused briefly to admire his walnut boards when they were displayed at the Crystal Palace in 1851. Now she was said to be haughty and austere. The feeling of awe increased when he entered the vast enclosure of ancient buildings and towers, courtyards and gardens overlooking the Thames River. Sentries in bearskin hats, their faces rigid and expressionless, stood guard at the entrance. Scarlet-clad servants led the party along seemingly endless corridors to Victoria's sitting room.

Josiah and Nancy had a vague blurred impression of heavy damask draperies and walls literally almost covered with pictures. The Queen, seated on a sofa upholstered in crimson, was in black except for a white tulle cap worn over graying hair parted in the middle. Surrounded by cushions, she appeared even smaller than she actually was. Her chubby hands, heavily ringed, rested in her lap.

"Why, Mr. Henson," she said, "I expected you to be an old man, but I am delighted to see you so well-preserved and good-looking."

Josiah bowed. "My Sovereign, that is what all the ladies tell me," he replied.

Though the Queen did not always appreciate facetious remarks, she seemed pleased by Josiah's quick reply. She asked him to sign his name in her private album, and she in turn presented him with an autographed portrait of herself. Members of her household staff, invited to meet the visitors, filed slowly by to shake hands. The next day, leading British newspapers printed in sentimental detail the story of the Reverend Henson's cordial reception. The account in the Birmingham *Daily Mail* read in part:

> He, the runaway slave, had lived to be entertained by Queen Victoria in her own royal castle. The whirling of time does indeed bring about its revenges, and not the least of them is the gracious and interesting ceremony performed at Windsor yesterday.

176

A Negro Preacher, bowed with age is he:
No sounding titles to his worth attest,
Yet in a land where all who tread are free
He, slave who was, is now its
Sov'reign's guest!

After their visit at Windsor, the Hensons went to Scotland, where they had the same cordial reception as in England. Josiah had grown accustomed to being introduced as "Uncle Tom," but it bothered him when some literal-minded readers called him an imposter. They had been deeply touched by the book's convincing description of Tom's death. How could it be, they wondered, that the original of that character was still alive.

Finally at a meeting in Glasgow, Josiah determined to set the record straight. His speech was quoted at length in the *Dumfries and Galloway Standard* for April 25, 1877. He told his audience:

"Now allow me to say that my name is not Tom, and never was Tom, and that I do not want to have any other name inserted in the newspapers for me than my own. My name is Josiah Henson, always was and always will be. I never change my colors. [Loud laughter.] You have read and heard some persons say that 'Uncle Tom is dead.' A great many have come to me in this country and asked me if I was not dead. I heard you were dead and read where you were. 'Well,' says I, 'I heard so too, but I never believed it yet. [Laughter.] I thought in all probability I would have found it out as soon as anybody else.' [Laughter.] It is not a very pleasant thing to me to hear that I am practicing an imposition upon the people. They have forgotten that Mrs. Stowe's *Uncle Tom's Cabin* is a novel; and it must have seemed a glorious finish

177

to that novel that she should kill her hero. Now you get the *Key* to *Uncle Tom's Cabin,* and I think you will there see me. [Laughter and applause.] You remember that when this novel of Mrs. Stowe's came out, it shook Americans almost out of their shoes, and out of their shirts. [Laughter.] They came to the conclusion that the whole thing was a falsehood, and so she brought out her *Key.* She told them where they would find a man named Josiah Henson. She said I was a venerable fellow, in which she was not much mistaken, for I am an old man preaching in Canada."

The audience applauded, and they smiled when he spoke of the color of his skin—"a substantial, fast color."

"The ladies must like it too," he added with a twinkle in his eyes, "since they like to dress in black."

Finally, he reminded his listeners that he was not responsible for anything that Mrs. Stowe had written in her novel, but only for what she had written about him in her *Key.* Though proud to be called "Uncle Tom" he also was proud of his own identity.

In the course of his talk, he repeated the words, "Josiah Henson is my name," and again he was applauded. The meeting ended—his last public appearance in the British Isles—with the audience joining in the chorus of "Glory, glory, hallelujah, freedom reigns today."

22

⚜

"I Always Was"

The Hensons sailed from Liverpool, April 28, 1877, with enough money to pay their debts and live in modest comfort. The months abroad had been a time of triumph that helped to compensate for earlier disappointments. Seated again by his own fireplace, Josiah could look up at the portrait of Queen Victoria that Nancy had hung in the place of honor. The grandchildren gathered to hear him tell of his adventures and to listen to the music box that friends across the ocean had sent especially for them. They were growing up in freedom in the province now known as Ontario. Life would be good to them. Toward the end it had been good to him.

Yet he had one longing still to be fulfilled. When Nancy wanted to spend Christmas with her sister in Baltimore, he proposed that they then go on to Washington. He was eager to see his old childhood home nearby in Maryland.

The city of Washington, when he and Nancy reached it the following March, looked different from the small town that he remembered. More than

179

a hundred and forty thousand people were living there by 1878. The orchard that once had covered part of the President's Square in front of the White House was now a park. On Josiah's last visit, James Monroe had been President. A familiar sight had been coffles of slaves being driven through the streets. Now Rutherford Hayes was the President of a nation that had outlawed slavery.

On those long-ago trips, when Josiah had brought Isaac Riley's farm produce to market, he had passed the White House often. When he returned with Nancy, they stood on the north portico with its tall white pillars waiting to be admitted as guests. Frederick Douglass, born in slavery, had been appointed United States Marshal for the District of Columbia, and he had written to the President in the Hensons' behalf. A year after they met Queen Victoria, they were about to be received by the elected head of their own native land.

"I called on His Excellency, President Hayes, in his office," Josiah said later, "while Mrs. Hayes showed my wife through the house. After a pleasant little chat about my trip across the water, he gave me a very cordial invitation to call again, should I ever pay another visit to the Capital."

For the drive to his old home, twelve miles away, Josiah hired a carriage. It traveled the same road over which he once had driven the Riley farm wagon, but when he reached the plantation he was shocked. Fields, pastures, and orchards were overgrown with weeds and underbrush. In the midst of this wilderness he located a little collection of mounds which was the family cemetery. A short distance from the others, he found his mother's grave.

He wept as he knelt beside it and recalled her grief when her children had been sold away from her. Except for him, she had never seen any of them again.

Josiah hardly expected to find Isaac Riley still living. He was not even sure that Isaac's grasping wife, Mathilda, would still be there, as he drove up the grass-grown road to the house. It looked shabby, and the black youth who suddenly appeared gazed open-mouthed at the handsome carriage. Yes, this was Mrs. Riley's house, he said, and went inside to announce the visitors.

"We went in," Josiah recalled, "and there was the old mistress sure enough. But instead of a young blooming woman of twenty, she was a poor fretful invalid of seventy. Her bed was in the old sitting room." Josiah went up to her and bowed.

"How do you do, madam," he said.

"I am poorly—poorly. I don't seem to know you."

"You have seen me many a time."

Suddenly she sat up in bed.

"Can it be Si?"

Years had passed since the Reverend Josiah Henson had been called by that old nickname, but he nodded.

"Not Si Henson surely. I cannot believe it. Let me feel your arms, then I shall know."

Josiah flung back his coat, and she felt the shoulders that had been broken as a result of defending her husband. She burst into tears.

"Indeed, it is Si! Oh, Si, your master is dead and gone. If only he were here, you would be good friends now, I know you would. You were always a good man, Si. I never blamed you for running away.

181

Oh, Si, don't you wish you could see your old master again?"

Josiah could not bring himself to say yes, but he talked with her calmly until she became quiet. She complained about how poor she was, with no slaves to work on the plantation. Isaac Riley had been a soldier in the War of 1812, and she would be entitled to a pension if only she had certain information that the government required. Though her husband had often talked of those days, she could not recall in what regiment he had served or the names of his officers. Did Si know? Josiah with his retentive memory was able to give her the information she would need.

She looked up at him gratefully. She saw not a slave but a dignified man in a black suit and white cravat.

"Why, Si, you are a gentleman," she told him.

"I always was," he said.

Epilogue

Josiah Henson preached his last sermon at the age of ninety-three. Harriet Beecher Stowe, twenty-three years younger, was to live on for another thirteen years, but Josiah's time was drawing to a close.

In May 1883, he lay dying in the frame cottage that one day would be known as the Uncle Tom's Cabin Museum. What his thoughts were no one could tell; he had so much to remember. He smiled at the members of his sorrowing family who had gathered around his bed.

"I could not stay if I would," he told them, "and I would not stay if I could."

A few days later people came from miles around to pay their final homage, and fifty wagons followed the hearse to the grave site where he lies buried. On the gray stone that marks his final resting-place were chiseled the words of an old hymn that expressed the enduring faith and optimism that had sustained him through a long productive life:

> There is a land of pure delight
>   Where saints immortal reign;
> Infinite day excludes the night,
>   And pleasures banish pain.

Acknowledgments

The dialogue in this book is based primarily on Josiah Henson's books but adapted to a style a man of the nineteenth century would have used in conversation. I have quoted from letters and biographies of Harriet Beecher Stowe, accounts by Henry Bleby and others who knew Josiah personally, as well as from contemporary newspaper accounts. Some of the quotations have been shortened and the spelling and punctuation modernized. I have called Josiah's brother "Jacob," since Henson in his own writings never mentioned his name. Certain descriptive details omitted by Henson in his own books—for instance, the kind of token given him by James Lightfoot when Josiah went to the rescue of the Lightfoot family—had to be supplied by the author.

The books and magazines consulted in presenting a picture of Josiah Henson and his times are too numerous to mention. In addition to the writings of Henson and Mrs. Stowe, the files of *The Liberator* were especially helpful, as were books by Winston J. Coleman, Jr., Benjamin Drew, Dwight L. Dumond,

Fred Landon, Gilbert Osofsky, Howard and Jane Pease, Benjamin Quarles, William Seibert, Robin Winks, and Carter Woodson. It was a privilege to have access to the Regional History Collection in the B. B. Weldon Library at the University of Western Ontario. Here I examined a remarkable two-volume doctoral dissertation on Negro Education in Ontario by Donald G. Simpson, head of the Office of International Education. Also helpful was the extensive collection of clippings, scrapbooks, letters, and other writings of the late Dr. Fred Landon, distinguished professor at the same university and an authority on the antislavery movement and the Civil War in the United States.

Grateful acknowledgment is made for courtesies shown the author by Edward Phelps, Regional History/Rare Book Librarian, University of Western Ontario; Elizabeth Spicer, librarian in the London Room, Humanities Area, London, Ontario, Public Library; librarians in the Massachusetts Historical Society and the Boston Public Library; Herbert Davis of the Library of Congress; Mrs. Mabel Turner, resident manager of the Montgomery County Historical Society, Rockville, Maryland; and to L. D. Thomson, curator of the Uncle Tom's Cabin Museum, Dresden, Ontario.

I also enjoyed the morning spent with Stanley R. Smith of Ingersoll, Ontario, who as a boy had attended school with some of the Henson descendants. I remember with special pleasure an evening with Mrs. Margaret Landon, widow of the late Dr. Fred Landon, who was generous in sharing her memories of her husband's work. The cooperation of Mrs. Vera

186

Gillham, who prepared the manuscript for the printer, is much appreciated. Special thanks are due Mrs. Esther M. Douty, author and an authority on the period of history covered in this story of Josiah Henson, for her many helpful suggestions.